Simplicity, Love and Justice

A discussion course

First Published 2004
Reprinted 2005

ISBN 1.904074.63.4

Published by:

Alpha International,
Holy Trinity Brompton,
Brompton Road,
London,
SW7 1JA
England.

Tel: 0845 644 7544
Email: publications@alpha.org

Contents

'People on the course were immediately stimulated and challenged.'

Preface

As a result of the ministry of God's Holy Spirit, more people today seem to be sensing a desire to get out into their local community and make some practical difference to the lives of those around them. But often we are not sure how to start, or whether the money or the time or the things which we want to give will in fact achieve anything worthwhile; and, too, we see so much that needs to be done, and so many people who need what little we have to give, that we do not know where to start and as a result we do not start at all. Yet the desire to see social change comes from the Holy Spirit; so it is supremely the work of the church.

James Odgers, who has been a friend and a leader in our church for many years, started Besom on his return from working with Jackie Pullinger-To in Hong Kong over 16 years ago. He remains closely involved with Jackie's work and shares her heart for the poor.

He set out to provide us here with a variety of practical ways in which people could be equipped to take the first steps across the bridge towards those in need. His aim was to establish a professional and efficient structure within which giving could become fun, easy, rewarding and safe for everyone. James practised as a solicitor in the City of London for eight years before becoming a banker for seven years. He is now a farmer in Somerset. This background, coupled with a compassion for the poor and the marginalised, makes him the ideal person to be running Besom, combining, as he does, a love for people with a solid understanding of the way things work in the world.

We here have watched with excitement as Besom has grown, and we have been thrilled to discover how many of us have been enabled by Besom to get going at any one time. For example, many of the home groups now go out regularly to paint or decorate the flats of those who live in shabby or degrading housing, to help with gardening, to befriend the lonely, the elderly or the fearful. So many of those who take part in such projects come back very moved and with tales of lives transformed – often their own – and of their home groups becoming stronger and more closely-knit. It is true to say that those for whom least is done are often most grateful; certainly we have found that the work of Besom has enriched the lives of all of us both as individuals and as a church.

Working with the poor can sometimes be thought of as only for a select few. But most of us recognise deep down that Jesus wants us all to be involved; Besom makes this possible. The different services offered by Besom mean that we can now all be involved whether in the home or in the office, whatever age we are and whether we have a lot or a little to give. Besom has increasingly become a part of our culture so we know it works in practice. It has proved itself to be a useful and necessary tool. Now, the BIAS project aims to resource any church or fellowship wanting to start a Besom themselves and to get the benefit of the lessons that have been learned along the way.

We here at Holy Trinity Brompton are humbly proud to be associated with James Odgers and Besom; I feel confident that it is at the very centre of God's hopes for his church today. Anything we can do to get involved with the poor will, I know, be more than rewarded both in this world and the next and I know that Besom itself will continue to give every encouragement and support. To this end, this book is only a start but a very important start. I am deeply grateful to have the chance to commend the work wholeheartedly through this preface.

Sandy Millar

Vicar of Holy Trinity Brompton
and Priest-in-Charge of the Tollington Team in North London

Foreword

I saw the first, faint outline of the notice some time ago. It was clearly there – some way along the narrow road that leads to life – so it was unavoidable. It was just this side of a gateway leading on to the next part of my journey on that road. In some ways, even though I have a strong and passionate faith in Jesus, it could not have been a more unwelcome notice coming from my background in the UK: white, middle-class, male, public school, Oxford, City lawyer, banker and now farmer. I walked towards it reluctantly.

The writing on the notice was clear too. It said that as I passed through the gateway, I would begin to hear, as never before, the cries of the poorest and the most excluded on this planet – cries for food, cries for mercy, cries for rest, cries for justice, cries for love. My love.

I have passed through the gateway now and stand the far side of it. For the time being, at least, I find that I cannot close my ears to those cries. They are not deafening so much as urgent, heart-rending and desperate. And my heart is full of questions about the character of the God of love and justice, whom we worship, and about what it means to love him. And to love our neighbour as we love ourselves.

God seems to be talking today to many people around the world who have passed through this gateway so I thought I would put some materials together to describe the lie of the land as I perceive it stretching out in front of me, in case this might help others. And it is all ahead: I have scarcely begun to work out how to set about what comes next. Please do not think otherwise. Of one thing I am sure: if the body of Christ in this country is ever to see our God heal this land of ours, this is a gateway through which he will be calling many more in the days to come.

The road ahead begins with this question: how can I live as I do when those who send up these agonised cries to an all-loving God live as they do?

My journey up to now has been a testimony to the extraordinary perseverance and love shown to me by God and by other people. God's love for you and me is a fiercely jealous one and he will pursue us relentlessly until we turn and requite it. Those he sent to tell me of his love faced what must have seemed an insurmountable task. At every step I would run off, at every mention of the Gospel I would smile knowingly and explain why it was not for me. And yet it was, of course – as it is for all of us.

After a forensic – and rather arrogant – examination of the evidence over several years (I was a rookie lawyer then, after all!) I discovered to my surprise and discomfiture that the Gospel record was a true one. This affected my life, however, not one jot because an intellectual faith is no faith at all. In Hong Kong I met several of those who had been healed immediately and painlessly of long-term heroin addiction in the ministry of Jackie Pullinger-To and I realised for the first time that if Jesus was alive today he would naturally be working in the same ways and in the same places as he did when he was here incarnate. The transformed lives of those men were a sufficient proof of that rather obvious fact. And it was then that my heart began to break for the poor and the marginalised. Jackie's description of poverty, by the way, is useful: 'Broadly speaking, we will interpret the poor as those who for some time are unable to free themselves from poverty and who need help.'

Yet I still continued along a path I chose rather than his path for me. Two years later he showed me how determined he is to ensure that we go his way and not ours. That unequal battle took me spiralling down to a very dark place from which I could not go on in my own strength. And I surrendered, at last, and then he began to show me some of the astonishing things he had prepared for me. At his behest, I left the law to go to work with Jackie and returned to found a sort of bank with three others in the City of London (that he has blessed outrageously) and to start The Besom (www.besom.com). I left the bank after seven years to establish FACE to Face, a ministry that encourages self-employment among the poor in our churches.

'One goes more quickly to heaven from a hut than from a palace.' St Francis of Assisi

Besom is a response to the chasm that yawns ever wider between those of us who have, and can give, and those in need. It provides a tiny and rickety bridge to help us to cross that chasm and it challenges us as we go.

Often at Besom, people come back from the other side of the divide not just excited about the transformation in the lives of those they have assisted but also with questions about their response to what they have seen, often for the first time: people living in circumstances of extreme degradation; people so lonely they are on the verge of suicide; people hungry for food and for love. Their love. And the questions inexorably lead on to other questions – not about the people on the receiving end but about us, those of us who have and can give. Poverty is not primarily about the poor but about those of us who have the means to alleviate it. Exclusion is not about the excluded but about we who do the excluding. Marginalisation is not about the marginalised but about we who do the marginalising. Love – the sort of love that God the Father showed when he sent his Son to die for you and for me, that sort of love – is said by St Paul to have been poured into our hearts by his Spirit. Yet if it has been, as St John wrote, then we are bound to assist all those in need that we come across and whose needs we can diminish or assuage. If we do not, he asks, 'how can the love of God be in' us? How indeed!

John Stott, in *New Issues Facing Christians Today*, writes that 'simple living is not incompatible with [the] careful enjoyment' of whatever we have been given, or have earned with the gifts and talents God has given us.[1] I agree up to a point (for Jesus came that we might have life in all its fullness) but that enjoyment – in the sense of using for our own pleasure – will inevitably be subordinate to the demands of love and these are never 'careful' in the worldly sense of prudent but instead often require the imprudent use – even the seeming waste – of time and resources, the going of extra miles and the incurring of cost or even sacrifice. So love will reduce what there is to 'enjoy' and thus will – must perforce – lead us to a much more simple (but rich) lifestyle, closer to that which would reflect more obviously a deep compassion for those in need. That way, and only that way, lies integrity. These materials are designed to assist us to discover a response to the love he showed us; a response to the cries of those in need; a response to that inevitable question 'How can I ..., when they...?'

What follows has only come about thanks to two extraordinary people. The first is Perry-May Ward, who now works at St Paul's, Hammersmith, having previously worked at the World's End Community Church in Chelsea, London. She travelled with my family and me in 1998 and 1999 during our research into different ways in which people sought to alleviate poverty in the most degrading and hopeless parts of the world. She began assembling these materials on our return, before she moved to work on a very difficult council housing estate in the UK. Ruth Valerio took over the task in Spring 2000 having left her role as Head of Social Responsibility at the Evangelical Alliance. Ruth and her husband Greg are behind Cred (Christian Research, Education and Development; www.cred.tv), an organisation that 'aims to resource and empower people who have a desire to see a more equitable and just world'. Ruth has also written a book: 'L is for Lifestyle: Christian living that doesn't cost the earth'. Perry-May, Ruth and Greg seem to me to have rushed through the gateway long since with a joy and determination that show a level of faith and trust that I can only long for.

It is really Perry-May and Ruth who, between them, have written and sorted the materials which follow and turned them into ten moderately bite-sized chunks. Frankly, they have done far more, far more effectively, than I. Everything that is good and right is down to them. The mistakes, omissions, non sequiturs and tendentious comments, of which there are many, are mine.

I would add my thanks to Sandy Millar and the rest of the team at Holy Trinity Brompton. They have been unswervingly generous over the years as Besom and FACE to Face have got up and running and have ever been a source of love and good advice. They are an amazing crowd and if you have yet to go on an Alpha course, despite all they have done to encourage you to do so, may I recommend that you hasten to the nearest one (alphacourse.org). I am also grateful to Miles and Deborah Protter, whose excited response to, and detailed comments on, the first draft of the materials encouraged me to persevere. My thanks too to Toria Gray, Julia Evans and Sarah Bibby at Holy Trinity Brompton, who have taken on the task of getting the materials from a recalcitrant Besom computer to the point of publication, and to all of those, too numerous to mention by name, who tested the materials and fed back their comments.

'We must be the change we wish to see in the world.' Gandhi

Four final points: first, I have not attempted to address specifically two fundamental issues both of which are keys to an understanding of the great divisions in our nation – those of taste and class. This is not because they are unimportant but rather that I believe they will inexorably surface in most sessions. Secondly, I apologise for any material that has been taken from another source but has been inadequately acknowledged. This has not been done intentionally, and I am very happy to acknowledge any such plagiarism in a later edition. Thirdly, I hope that these materials are seen as the tools they are intended to be, no more and no less; we are all in process, all being transformed into his likeness. But the journey takes a lifetime. And, as I said at the outset, I am probably no further along the road than you. Lastly, discussion about living more simply has attracted others from different faiths (and none) for years. The body of Christ is late into the field, or peaked too early – perhaps in the thirteenth century! Some of the examples and quotations which follow might smack of the New Age, or of sandals and Woodstock, or of a 'back to the earth' movement, but they are nonetheless valid for all that if they provoke. The difference, very often, is that the New Age seeks the divine within, whereas we worship and follow the model of a God Incarnate.

James Odgers

Founder
The Besom
Spring 2004

'People enjoyed discussing the issues the course raised and found it possible to relate to them, despite all being at very different stages of their Christian lives. The overwhelming positive is the quality and breadth of the materials. You could not fault the course for not being practical enough! Another real bonus has been that the course has given us a vocabulary for challenging each other about our lifestyles, how we spend our money, etc., which we previously lacked.'

'What is my new desert? The name of it is compassion. There is no wilderness so terrible, so beautiful, so arid and so fruitful as the wilderness of compassion. It is the only desert that shall truly flourish like the lily. It shall become a pool, it shall bud forth and blossom and rejoice with joy. It is in the desert of compassion that the thirsty land turns into springs of water, that the poor possess all things.' Thomas Merton

INTRODUCTION

'He has showed you, O people, what is good. And what does the Lord require of you? To act justly and to love mercy and to walk humbly with your God' (Micah 6:8)

About the Material

Welcome to these materials on simpler living. We are excited that you have decided to join us in looking at the issues involved.

We live at an extraordinary time in history when communication and technology are advancing rapidly, medical science is achieving near miracles and consumer choice is at its highest. Yet global inequality is at an extreme. In light of this we have to ask ourselves the question that Micah asked, 'What does the Lord require of me?' In our world today what does it mean to act justly and to love mercy? How do we walk humbly with our God? These are difficult questions that speak into every aspect of our lives and every decision that we make, so our faith demands that we work hard at exploring the answers.

Many people today in the West are recognising that something is wrong with the way they live their lives. These materials are a tool for those who are ready to talk about change. It is an opportunity to discover what is good and true.

In the 1970s, the concept of living a simple life came to prominence in the church with the Lausanne Covenant's declaration on simple lifestyle. This said:

... all of us are shocked by the poverty of millions and disturbed by the injustices which cause it. Those of us who live in affluent circumstances accept our duty to develop a simple lifestyle in order to contribute more generously to both relief and evangelism.[2]

From this statement a consultation process emerged that culminated in 'An Evangelical Commitment to Simple Lifestyle' in the eighties. It is a very helpful document that we recommend you read. It can be found as an Occasional Paper on Lausanne's website, www.gospelcom.net/lcwe.[3] The challenge to us all, though, is how to move from such a declaration to its personal application in each of our lives.

It is sometimes said that simple living is a luxury that only the middle classes can afford. It is certainly true that there will be a number of challenges throughout this material that will only apply to certain types of people and churches. Sensitivity will need to be shown towards those in the group who may not be in paid employment or may be struggling on a low income. However, regardless of employment or income, we are all rich when compared with the vast majority of people around the world. Therefore there is much in these materials that can and should be embraced by almost everyone in the West. 'As with all other aspects of simplifying, going against the grain takes a little more creativity and energy, but the results are well worth it.' [4]

With all this in mind, *Simplicity, Love and Justice* is designed to help church groups look at different aspects of their lives and re-evaluate the decisions they have made and the values that they have accepted.

'Son, now I will teach you the way of peace and of true liberty. Try, my son to do the will of another rather than your own. Always choose to have less rather than more. Always seek to take the last place, and to be subject to everyone. Always desire and pray that the will of God be perfectly fulfilled in you. Behold, a man so disposed enters in the land of peace and rest.'
Thomas à Kempis, **The Imitation of Christ**

In summary, the aim of the material is to help us:

- **Work out the relationship between our faith and our lifestyle**
- **Gain a biblical understanding of the issues involved in simplicity**
- **Become more familiar with the social and global context within which we live**
- **Develop community and support**

As groups tackle sensitive issues together, the overriding atmosphere should be one of grace, not legalism, love, not criticism. There will be sessions and exercises that will no doubt provoke a reaction in us or others and we should allow the Holy Spirit to encourage and, where necessary, to convict, rather than jump in with any condemnation of our own. No one can achieve true holiness on earth, but all can start to move towards it. The exciting promise for every believer is that by no action of our own but rather by the power of his Spirit working within us, we are being transformed into the Lord's likeness with ever increasing glory (2 Corinthians 3:18). Perhaps reflecting upon these materials will enable us to be more open to this process!

Do I have to study this in a group?

The decision to live more simply is a personal one, but difficult decisions made within an encouraging environment are much easier to put into practice than decisions made alone. Going against the flow is never easy and therefore studying as a group is the best way to make progress.

Community is central to the vision of voluntary simplicity and the Christian faith offers an opportunity to create communities with Jesus at the heart and where others are more important than ourselves. Doris Janzen Longacre said that in American society today 'no one feels obligated to catch us if we fall. We've traded the restrictions of tightly-laced communities for a lonely freedom'.

Loneliness is one of the worst forms of poverty in the developed world. By studying together we not only learn from one another, but we create lasting friendships. Through a group we not only experience community, we begin to define it!

How to use the material

This course is designed for discussion in small groups, ideally of around five people who know one another. There is an expectation that group members will commit themselves fully to the course. It is of no fixed length, as different groups may need different amounts of time to build trust and confidentiality, and an atmosphere without legalism or judgmentalism. This course is a very personal journey and we come with different histories and experiences that mould our approaches and make different things important to us. As Ron Sider warns: 'There is no one lifestyle that is right for all Christians in one country, or even for all Christians in one congregation. There must be room for the variety and diversity so gorgeously displayed in the creation.'[5] Perhaps it might be helpful for everyone to start off by sharing that part of their 'story' relevant to the course as a way of building links and understanding. As Atticus says in To Kill a Mockingbird: 'You never understand a person until you have put on their shoes and walked around in them.'

It is up to each group to establish their own guidelines for discussions and to decide how long they spend on each subject. There may be some issues that are not relevant to a particular group. It is recommended, as far as possible, that while there may be one person who acts as overall group facilitator, a different person leads through each meeting to help build a sense of group ownership. Please note that the role of the facilitator is to lead people through the suggested format. There is no expectation that the facilitator must deliver a short (still less a long) talk!

'To build choices on anything less than love for our sisters and brothers is to make life another in a string of competitions. Justice is and must be a relational issue. Its only authentic root is intense love.'
Dee Dee Risher. Northwest Earth Institute

A suggested format for each meeting:

Meal
The evening could start with a simple meal. Sharing food together is also an opportunity to chat and relax together.

Prayer and worship
On this spiritual journey there is an increasing need for the power of the Holy Spirit to be present in all that we look at. Therefore prayer and worship are key elements in working through the course. Set prayers and worship times will not be provided so it will be up to you to bring them in as you feel appropriate.

Feedback
Except for the first meeting, give people an opportunity to say how they got on with their action points and /or homework from the previous week. This is an essential element of the course because it is a helpful way of building-in a level of accountability to one another and ensuring that people actually carry out what they have said they will do!

Goals
Consider the goals for the meeting – it is not necessary to achieve all of them and you may find that others emerge.

Reading
A personal commitment to the course involves the understanding that each person in the group should read the material before the meeting. This gives an opportunity for members already to have thought through some of the issues before discussing them in the group.

Discussion
Have a time of discussion. There are suggested questions but, again, you are entirely free to create your own. There are deliberately more questions than you will be able to discuss in one meeting so you can choose which ones you look at – but don't let that be an excuse to duck the harder questions! It might be helpful for the facilitator to ask if there are any questions that others would particularly like to pursue during the discussion.

Action
Decide on at least one action that each member will take in their lives each time and remember to feed back every week. The action points are suggestions, not legalistic prescriptions, and individuals must feel free to choose to do something else if appropriate.

Homework
These exercises are designed to help individuals assess themselves and take challenges further. Time spent on these during the week will ensure that each group member gains the maximum from the course.

With this format in mind, it will be clear that each group member will need to set aside time between meetings to think through the previous session thoroughly and prepare for the next. It may also be worth considering doing the last session as a weekend away, as a chance to spend time with one another, reflecting on what the Spirit has been teaching the group over the weeks, to pray for its members and to discuss how they may support one another in any future commitments they feel led to make.

'The emphasis is practical and people have been jogged into 'doing' something about it all.'

'To live contentedly, we must learn to accept and live in harmony with who we are – not who we want to be or feel we need to be, not who our co-worker is. We must accept our gifts and our flaws.'
Dee Dee Risher, Northwest Earth Institute

Further Reading and Resources

At the end of each session you will find two or three specific books, relevant to the topic, and then there is a full bibliography at the end of the course. Website addresses for useful organisations are given throughout the material and a few extras are given at the end, along with the website addresses/contact details for the organisations related to the authors (for a more comprehensive list and contact details, see the end of each chapter in R. Valerio, *L is for Lifestyle: Christian Living that Doesn't Cost the Earth).*

A Note on Timings

We have chosen not to give timings. It is recommended that the meetings last around an hour and a half, but it is up to the group how much time is spent on each section. While most time will be spent on the discussion, it may be, for instance, that on one particular week more time needs to be spent praying for one another (in the light of the issues raised), or perhaps studying a biblical passage to gain a deeper understanding before looking at questions of application. There are no rules! Above all, make this experience a positive one – full of laughter and fun amid the challenges.

It is important, again, that each member of the group is encouraged, no matter how they react to the issues. No one should be criticised and comparisons between group members are particularly unhelpful (and miss the point of an essentially personal quest). Don't move on to the next subject until you feel ready to tackle it. You may find that you stay on one subject for a few weeks without looking at any others.

We would love to hear from you. On your journey of discovery you will discover things that are not covered by this discussion course. Please write to us (simplicity@besom.com.) and tell us what you learn so that we can include your experiences in later editions.

'... Become nothing before God, learn to keep silent; in this silence is the beginning which is first to seek God's kingdom'
Soren Kierkegaard, quoted in Richard Foster, Celebration of Discipline

SESSION ONE

What is simplicity?

'If any one of you has material possessions and sees a brother or sister in need but has no pity on them, how can the love of God be in you?' (1 John 3:17)

Goals

- To understand as a group what voluntary simplicity is.
- To set some personal goals.
- To set some group ground rules.

Reading

> 'Therefore I tell you, do not worry about your life, what you will eat or drink or about your body, what you will wear. Is not life more important than clothes? Look at the birds of the air; they do not sow or reap or store away in barns, and yet your heavenly Father feeds them. Are you not much more valuable than they? Who of you by worrying can add a single hour to your life?
>
> And why do you worry about clothes? See how the lilies of the field grow. They do not labour or spin. Yet I tell you that not even Solomon in all his splendour was dressed like one of these. If that is how God clothes the grass of the field, which is here today and tomorrow is thrown into the fire, will he not much more clothe you, O you of little faith? So do not worry, saying "What shall we eat?" or "What shall we wear?" for the pagans run after all these things, and your heavenly Father knows that you need them. But seek first his kingdom and his righteousness, and all these things will be given to you as well' (Matthew 6:25–33).

Simplicity is not a word we tend to hear much these days. If we do it is often used in connection with an interior design that might be simple to look at but expensive to obtain! Certainly, it is rare that the subject of simplicity is raised within the body of Christ. And yet, as we saw in the introduction, simplicity is an essential part of the Christian life and also has the potential to speak directly to our society.

Henry Thoreau, one of the great writers on this issue, said that 'a person is rich in proportion to the things they can leave alone' and, in many ways, this sums up what simple living is all about. Partly, it's about our choices. As we look at our lives, do we know how we've ended up living how we're living and why? What choices have we made that control our present lifestyle? When we wanted that new house or car were we aware that the trade-off would mean working longer hours to pay for them and seeing less of the people we love? Too often we find ourselves on the treadmill of life, paying the consequences for choices we hardly knew we were making.

Simple living is about stopping that treadmill and giving ourselves the space to choose how we want to live our lives. There are many voices around us that tell us that happiness is to be found in good clothes and nice jewellery; in a job that commands respect; in crashing out in front of the television set in order to recover; in having a busy diary. Simplicity asks us to sit and listen to those other whispers inside us that we seldom have the time to hear. It helps us discover the happiness that comes – not from having an abundance of money and things – but from having the space for intimacy in our friendships, space for ourselves and, primarily, the space for God.

'I cannot tell you with truth that when this belief came to me I discarded everything immediately. I must confess to you that progress at first was slow... it was also painful at the beginning. But as days went by I saw I had to throw overboard many other things which I used to consider as mine, and a time came when it became a matter of positive joy to give up those things... A great burden fell off my shoulders and I felt I could now walk with ease... The possession of anything then became a troublesome thing and a burden'.
Gandhi, on simplicity.

Too often our days are spent thinking about the future: we drive the children to school or drive to work while planning what we will do that day, on auto-pilot, hardly noticing anything or anybody we drive past. As we talk to a friend on the phone we are thinking what we will have for lunch and fail to hear what she is really saying. We shove a plastic container in the microwave and eat its contents while thinking about a later meeting and miss the pleasure of eating good, simple food. Simple living is about being joyfully aware of what we do and why we do it. We can live in the present as well as the future; having the room to savour each moment of our lives.

When approaching such an issue, we should always look at Jesus' own words and his attitude to life.[6] The Sermon on the Mount makes it clear that the key point in every aspect of our lives is to seek first the kingdom of God and its righteousness and then everything else will follow naturally. Jesus is to be our cornerstone and every aspect of our lives should hinge upon him.

Nothing must come before the seeking of the kingdom of God, including the desire for a simple lifestyle. As Richard Foster says, 'focus on the Kingdom produces the inward reality, and without the inward reality we will degenerate into legalistic trivia. Nothing else can be central. The desire to get out of the rat race cannot be central, the redistribution of the world's wealth cannot be central, the concern for ecology cannot be central. Seeking first God's kingdom and the righteousness, both personal and social, of that kingdom is the only thing that can be central in the spiritual discipline of simplicity'.[7]

Simplicity is something every Christian should take seriously. It is deeply rooted in the Bible and as followers of Jesus we see it perfectly modelled in his own lifestyle. Simplicity is not a modern response to environmental issues but a natural and necessary response to the good news of Jesus Christ. It involves removing barriers which restrict us from touching God personally and which also restrict us from meeting the needs of people around us. By embracing simplicity we achieve a higher quality of life in which our values are placed in people rather than material possessions. However, we need to be aware that moving towards simplicity will require not only going against the materialism of our society, but also against where this materialism has crept into our churches and church groups.

For simplicity to be both fulfilling and sustaining, one must choose it. To some there may be no appeal to living simply and the best reason for not leading a simple life is not wanting to! Meaningful simple living requires a person willing it for themselves, as does the nature and degree of simplification. Simplicity is more a state of mind than a particular standard of living. All Christians should consciously prioritise their activities with God thus developing a wholeness in their walk with Christ and a holiness in their approach to decision-making.

Money or possessions or activities themselves do not corrupt simplicity, but the love of money, the craving for possessions and the prison of activities do. Knowing the difference between personal trappings and personal traps, therefore, is a key to mastering the art of simpler living.

Richard Foster says that the Christian discipline of simplicity 'is an inward reality that results in an outward lifestyle' and both are essential: 'We deceive ourselves if we believe we can possess the inward reality without its having a profound effect on how we live.'[8] However, the reverse is also true. The outward action without the inward reality can lead to guilt and legalism. These materials are primarily designed to tackle the outward questions and focus on material, rather than spiritual, poverty, but we must remember at all times that they are part of our wider spirituality and walk with God. Thus throughout the course we must not neglect other disciplines such as prayer and fasting as we develop this particular discipline of simplicity.

Simple living enables us to get rid of the clutter that is in our lives so that we can hear the voice of God more clearly and serve him more readily. As we do that, we will discover what it really means to be rich, for simplicity is not about meanness and poverty, nor is it about unnecessary asceticism, but true life in all its abundance (John 10:10).

'Here is Edward Bear coming down the stairs now, bump bump bump bump on the back of his head. It is, as far as he knows, the only way of coming down the stairs but sometimes he feels there really is another way if he could only stop bumping for a moment and think of it.'
A. A. Milne, from Winnie-the-Pooh.

Discussion

- Read Matthew 6:19–34.
  - What do you understand from this passage about simplicity?
  - What are some of the things in your life that you worry about?
  - Jesus' words here form part of his larger teaching on discipleship and follow his teaching about prayer and fasting. We have seen that the outward expression of simplicity only comes from the inward reality. How can you keep that balance over these next weeks?
  - How do you feel you are putting the injunction to *'seek first the kingdom of God'* into practice in your life?

- Make a list of all of the things that are available to each one of us without money coming into the equation at all – the things that no amount of money could buy even if we had an infinite amount. Salvation is not a bad place to start. ('Coral, green and grey,' continued Muzzlehatch... 'are these the colours of the sky tonight? Do you pay, my Dears, to see the sunset? Ain't the sunset free?' – Mervyn Peake, Titus Alone).

- Discuss together why you want to be part of your group and want to study these materials.

- Consider how your life would be different if you lived with less. How is the idea attractive to you? Does the idea cause anxiety?

- Richard Foster makes ten suggestions to help us begin to receive the full benefits of simplicity:
  1. Buy things for their usefulness rather than their status.
  2. Reject anything that is producing an addiction in you. Learn to distinguish between a real psychological need, like cheerful surroundings, and an addiction.
  3. Develop the habit of giving things away.
  4. Refuse the propaganda of the custodians of modern gadgetry.
  5. Learn to enjoy things without owning them.
  6. Develop a deeper appreciation for Creation.
  7. Look with a healthy scepticism at all 'buy now, pay later' schemes.
  8. Obey Jesus' instructions about plain, honest speech: 'let what you say simply be "yes" or "no"; anything more than this comes from evil' (Matthew 5:37).
  9. Reject anything that breeds the oppression of others.
  10. Shun anything that distracts you from seeking first the Kingdom of God.[9]

Which ones strike you as particularly interesting or challenging?

- How do you feel about being a minority?

- Look again at the introduction and agree some ground rules for your times together over the coming weeks. Is everyone happy with the suggested format?

'We just finished the Simplicity course. We used it with a group of mums during the day time and it was a brilliant success, challenging all our mindsets and creating a lot of change!'

'Many of them had a better time than they ever had in their lives because they were discovering the new freedom – the less you need, the freer you become. They discovered and kept discovering that they were carrying far too much baggage and so they dropped pieces right and left. And the more they dropped, the happier they became... and when they thought they had dropped nearly everything, they discovered that they were still needing and using and wasting more than the great majority of mankind.'
E. F. Schumacher describing people who, by conscious choice, were learning to live with less.

Action

Decide prayerfully what you will put into practice this week. Be prepared to report back on your progress however successful it was. These personal goals could be from the list of 'Five simple things you could do right now' below, or from Foster's ten suggestions or anything else of your choice.

Five simple things you can do right now

1. Think of a neighbour or a friend who needs some help, whether financially or in some other way, and do something to meet that need this week.
2. Set aside two half-hour periods during this week when you can have some space for sitting quietly.
3. Go through your clothes and give away anything you have not worn over the past year.
4. Look at the amount of packaging involved in the food you buy and work on reducing it to a bare minimum.
5. Do not use your car this week for any journey under two miles.

Homework

Take some time, an afternoon or even a whole weekend, perhaps with some friends, to talk about your sense of purpose in life and how you want to spend your time here in this life. Then commit to praying about it regularly and start to see how you could bring about change.
OR: Set some personal goals :

Steps I can take to move toward simplicity

THINGS TO CHANGE	IMMEDIATELY	WITHIN SIX MONTHS
Daily practice or habit		
Possessions		
Non-material attachments		
Use of money		
Work		
Use of time		
Shopping habits		
Attitude towards social pressure		
Habits that affect the environment negatively		
Building my community		
Other		

'Poverty was to St Francis a treasure – not an evil to be endured, but a priceless gem to be possessed.'

Prayer

Take some time to discuss how people are feeling so far. Meeting together to look at these subjects takes courage and people may well be feeling nervous or vulnerable. Close your meeting by praying for one another.

Further reading

- Richard Foster, *Celebration of Discipline* (Hodder & Stoughton, 1989).
- Richard Foster, *Freedom of Simplicity* (HarperCollins, 1989).
- Michael Schut (ed.), *Simpler Living: Compassionate Life* (Thomas More Press, 1999).

'When the church commits itself to a pattern of corporate life based on radical biblical principles, it immediately challenges the moral, political, economic and social structures of the world around it...only in this way will the proclamation of the gospel make much impact amongst the vast majority of people who, at this moment, are thoroughly disillusioned by the church as an institution.'
David Watson – Discipleship

Notes

Notes

SESSION TWO

Time

'There is a time for everything and a season for every activity under heaven…' (Ecclesiastes 3:1).

Goals

'I enjoyed it – I enjoy this full-on, confrontational challenge stuff as then something tends to click inside my head and heart!'

- To consider whether our time is spent on what God values most.
- To consider alternatives to a fast pace of life.

Reading

'There remains then, a Sabbath-rest for the people of God; for anyone who enters God's rest also rests from their own work, just as God did from His. Let us, therefore, make every effort to enter that rest, so that no one will fall by following their example of disobedience.' (Hebrews 4:9–11)

Time is God's creation and his gift to us. He has given it to us to enjoy and to use for his service. It is given to each of us in completely equal amounts and it is hence our responsibility how we choose to conduct ourselves as stewards of that allotted time. Simple living allows time to be the most rewarding and beautiful possession that we have, helping us reach a place of wholeness and awareness both of ourselves and of God.

And yet, 'I haven't got the time' is one of the most frequently heard complaints of our society. Listen to this description of our lives:

> Capitalism has brought a dramatically increased standard of living, but at the cost of a much more demanding worklife. We are eating more, but we are burning up those calories at work. We have colour televisions and compact disc players, but we need them to unwind after a stressful day at the office. We take vacations, but we work so hard throughout the year that they become indispensable to our sanity. The conventional wisdom that economic progress has given us more things as well as more leisure is difficult to sustain.[10]

As a result, many around us are suffering. Stress is now one of the biggest problems in our society, resulting in millions of pounds lost through days off work and medical bills. Much of this has come about because of increased pressure at work with many more demands being placed on us and an expectation of increasingly longer hours.

Sleep is one of the casualties of this and many people are not able to get their required amount each night, thus leading to sleep deprivation problems. It is not uncommon to hear of people lying awake in bed in the early hours, unable to sleep, because of work issues going round and round in their heads.

Fundamentally, it is relationships that suffer. Families are placed under increasing amounts of strain as both partners go out to paid work in order to bring home enough money. An increase in shift work only exacerbates the problem. Children often have to let themselves in after school and look after themselves in the absence of their working parent or parents. Friendships and caring for one another also struggle under the weight of time pressures. We simply do not have the time for one another. When we are not at work we want to relax and unwind. To cook a meal for a sick friend or visit a lonely neighbour requires more of us than we are able to give.

'God, in all besides bounteous and magnificent, teaches us, by the wise parsimony of his providence, frugality and foresight in the use of time, since he gives it but by single moments: the first has disappeared before its successor is in our grasp; and whether it will please him to give or retain the next, it is beyond our knowledge.' Archbishop Fenelon

This was exemplified by a group of young workers in the City of London who used to meet regularly. Their common complaint was that they had no time to do anything other than work in the investment banks, the law firms and the accountants' practices upon which the City's renown is based. They would tell of how little time they had to spend with their loved ones or with God, and of how they saw their children only at weekends. How many were called into those all-consuming jobs? In the coming weeks we will look more deeply at the subjects of money and work. God might call a person into such a job, but both the Bible and history would suggest that this type of vocation is more rare than we might like to think.

What is clear is that things are only going to get worse. As Tom Sine says, 'that means we will have less time for family and friends, less time to pray and study Scripture and less time to volunteer to address the mounting needs of the poor in our societies'. [11]

Consider Harry Chapin's song, *'Cat's in the Cradle'*

My child arrived just the other day,
He came to the world in the usual way –
But there were planes to catch and bills to pay
He learned to walk while I was away
And he was talking fore I knew it and as he grew he'd say,

I'm gonna be like you, Dad
You know I'm gonna be like you.

And the cat's in the cradle and the silver spoon
Little boy blue and the man in the moon
When you comin' home, Dad

I don't know when but we'll get together then –
You know we'll have a good time then

My son turned ten just the other day
He said, Thanks for the ball, Dad, com'on let's play
Can you teach me to throw?
I said not today, I got a lot to do
He said That's okay
And he walked away but his smile never dimmed
It said I'm gonna be like him, yeah
You know I'm gonna be like him

And the cat's in the cradle and the silver spoon
Little boy blue and the man in the moon
When you comin' home, Dad
I don't know when but we'll get together then –
You know we'll have a good time then

Well, he came home from college just the other day
So much like a man I just had to say
Son, I'm proud of you, can you sit for a while
He shook his head and said with a smile –
What I'd really like, Dad, is to borrow the car keys
See you later, can I have them please?

When you comin' home, Son?
I don't know when but we'll get together then
You know we'll have a good time then

I've long since retired, my son's moved away
I called him up just the other day
I said I'd like to see you if you don't mind
He said, I'd love to, Dad – if I can find the time

You see my new job's a hassle and the kids have the flu,
But it's sure nice talkin to you, Dad
It's been nice talking to you

And as I hung up the phone, it occurred to me –
He'd grown up just like me; my boy was just like me. [12]

How have we got ourselves into this state? Our experience of time has become inextricably linked to our consumer culture and most of us now realise that we are paying an unforeseen price for the standard of living we have chosen. One of the greatest ironies of time is that it often seems to be directly disproportional to the amount of money we have. Hence, while we are all granted it in equal proportions, time is actually one of the great dividers. It distinguishes between those who spend time to save money and those who spend money to save time. What is important to grasp is that 'the new materialism is to do with our attitude to time'.[13] Time has now become a status symbol, like money. Many of us measure our worth by how busy we are and believe ourselves to be indispensable to all that goes on around us. Our wage-employment system often places an emphasis on the amount of hours we spend at work, rather than on the successful completion of a task.

'Be still and know that I am God'
(Psalm 46 v 10).

What we must grasp is that our use of time reflects the values of our lives. We will be spending a lot of time on this course looking at our values as Christians and how we connect to them through such things as our use of money, our work, or our concern for the environment. We first need to consider these values in respect of our time. We must be bold enough to ask ourselves whether or not we are truly living out God's values and, if not, what needs to change.

We are considering two topics. The first involves making changes so that we have the time simply to be. That is, to be with ourselves and with God. Time in this sense has been described as 'opening space in our lives for a greater awareness of God'.[14]

As we listen to God, in silence, solitude and contemplation, we consider before him the use of our time. Then we must be willing to make changes so that we have more time to do the things that we believe God wants us to do. This might involve spending time with him, with family, with friends in paid or unpaid employment, or in helping with community projects, or simply in taking time to relax.

Gerald May makes three suggestions about creating space: [15]

Firstly, he suggests looking for spaces that occur normally in our lives. That might mean a natural break after we have finished some work which could be expanded or maybe it is time in the shower or in the garden, or just before we settle down to sleep. May suggests thinking over a typical day in our mind and asking ourselves if there are moments which we immediately and automatically fill by turning on the TV or making ourselves a drink. It may be that, instead, we could extend those moments just a while longer and make them more 'intentional': moments to stop and be still.

Secondly, we should try to find the more regular set-aside spaces during the day that are 'simply and solely dedicated to just being'. To begin with these may just be a few minutes. However long they are, they are an opportunity, particularly at the start of the day, to take some space and establish ourselves with Jesus at the centre. Evening times can be a chance to reflect on what the day has held.

Finally, May recommends building longer spaces of authentic retreat into our lives. These may actually involve going away for a retreat or taking a day of quiet. It is worth finding out whether we find space more easily with other people or alone and this can help us decide if we should spend these times by ourselves or perhaps join with another group of people who have a similar desire.

As we talk about these things together we must remember that each one of us has different commitments and will be able to implement these suggestions at varying levels. Whatever we are able to do, our aim in all of this is to be getting our use of time under control so that it serves our kingdom values rather than those of the world; living intentionally in each moment of time. Let us conclude this section with Henri Nouwen's description of the contemplative life. He says that it is a life:

> 'in which time slowly loses its opaqueness and becomes transparent. This is often a very difficult and slow process, but full of re-creating power. To start seeing that the many events of our day, week or year are not in the way of our search for a full life, but the way to it, is a real experience of conversion.
>
> If we discover that writing letters, ... visiting people and cooking food are not a series of random events which prevent us from realising our deepest self, but contain in themselves the transforming power we are looking for, then we are beginning to move from time lived as chronos [events] to time lived as kairos [opportunity]'.[16]

Kosuke Koyama, an Asian theologian, describes God as the one who 'went so slow that he became nailed down in his search of man'. ...He describes what happens when free time changes to time as money:

We live in deeds, not years; in thoughts, not breaths;
In feelings, not in figures on a dial.
We should count time by heart throbs. He most lives
Who thinks most, feels noblest, acts the best.
Philip James Bailey

Time [in Asia] was traditionally experienced as being as unlimited as a loving mother's milk is unlimited to her baby. Time was generously given. It was not sold as pork chops are sold.... it was communal. Now, this has been changed without any consultation with us! ... Time is now located in the export-import companies, motorcycle manufacturers, stores and shops. ... It is now private business property. Once it was shared, now it is monopolised. Time does not heal us now. Time wounds us.[17]

Discussion

- Read Hebrews 4:1–11 and its discussion on Sabbath rest. Paul Mills says that the seventh day of Creation was never completed, suggesting that we are still living in the seventh day of divine 'rest' from creative activity.[18]
  How do you think that applies to us today?

- Who or what determines the pace of your life? What role does peer pressure play?

- Discuss what you spent your time on last week. Now identify how much of the decisions about where to spend your time came out of the expectations of modern culture and how much came out of the impulses of your faith?[19]

- Do you feel guilty if you are not as busy as those around you?

- Are you happy with your use of time? If not, discuss realistic ways in which you could use your time better.
  If it helps, look at the ideas below on how to slow down.

Possible things to do to slow down:

1. Prayerfully look at your commitments and activities, even the most trivial – is this really what God wants you to do with your time? No? Then act. Remember that just because you are doing something good does not mean that it is right. Learn to distinguish between what is important and what is urgent.

2. Get involved regularly with your community. For example, a local youth group, charity shop, college, retirement home, baby-sitting, doing someone's shopping or whatever it is you are interested in. Volunteer – give as much time away as you do money.

3. Plan life not time. Think regularly about what you want from your life (as opposed to how much you can 'get done').

4. Manage time organically. Time is uniform only to clocks. Our bodies keep irregular time, based on sunlight, temperature, and the uneven tempo of work and leisure that first sets our inner clocks. Get to know your own body clock, paying special attention to peak periods. Take advantage of peak periods in scheduling work: if you don't control your work schedule, try to negotiate one that allows this (it's in everyone's best interest!)

5. Decelerate. Don't make use of every minute; this only increases tension while reducing effectiveness. Rushing is addictive. Once hooked, it's hard to remember that the fastest way of doing things isn't always the best way. When hurried, ask yourself: 'Do I really need to rush? What's the worst thing that can happen to me if I don't? Is that worse than what it's costing me to hurry?' Distinguish between necessary haste (late for an appointment) and mere impatience (one hour photo developing).

6. Reduce awareness of time. How often do we really need to know what time it is? The fewer reminders we have of time, the better we can make this commodity serve rather than master us. Pay attention to how often you 'check the time'. Reduce such occasions to a minimum. Go watchless whenever possible.

> *'He (God) has contrived to gratify both tastes together in the very world He has made, by the union of change and permanence which we call Rhythm. He gives them the seasons, each season different yet every year the same, so that spring is always felt as a novelty yet always as the recurrence of an immemorial theme.'*
> *C. S. Lewis, The Screwtape Letters*

7. Learn to enjoy timeless (and free or inexpensive) activities like:

- acting
- baking
- bird and wildlife watching
- carpentry
- creative writing
- dancing
- visiting galleries
- needlework
- singing and music
- starting a book club
- storytelling
- hiking
- back-packing
- daydreaming
- camping
- conversation
- cycling
- drawing and painting
- gardening
- picnics, reading
- stargazing
- sport
- walking
- writing letters

The list is limited only by your imagination!

8. Plan evenings or weekends in!

9. Stop the future from impacting upon the present!

(Adapted from: The Northwest Earth Institute p. IV. Ralph Keyes, from: Timelock: How life got hectic and what you can do about it)

Other Ideas

1. Commit yourself to pray for 15 minutes a day. Set aside a specific time. For example, walking to the tube or bus stop, or in the shower. You don't have to be on your knees to pray effectively. Or, similarly, commit yourself to a period of silence each day.

2. As much as possible, walk or cycle rather than drive.

3. Offer to cook for your housemates one night a week.

4. If you have skills in areas like sewing, administration, accountancy, medicine, singing, art or teaching, then find a way of using your skill and give it away free.

Action

Spend one day without your watch on. What happened?

Be creative in the way you make gifts. Give presents that cost time rather than money. One person gave their friend the gift of time for their birthday and agreed to cook a meal and spend the evening with them once a month. There are many other things that can be given too!

'I don't have much money, but time is much more important than money to me. If I'm rich in time then I'm a wealthy man.'
Chris Yates, professional fisherman, and editor of fishing magazine Waterlog

Homework

Keep a log of your daily activities for at least one week in the time sheet provided in Appendix One, recording whatever you do each hour. Then using the Time Circles sheet in Appendix 2 make a pie chart for each day of how you spent your time, to give a clear overview.

1. Review the activities you have logged. How many of them bring the kind of reward and sense of satisfaction that you associate with the high points of your life?

2. If some activities are not rewarding or satisfying, what are they for? Are they necessary or could they be changed, reorganised or eliminated?

3. To what extent is your daily round of activity focused on aspects of material culture?
What rewards does this bring into your life?

4. To what extent does your daily activity help achieve your goals in life? Is it achieving someone else's goals?
If so, whose? Do you endorse those goals?

5. Design yourself a daily round of activities that would bring you closer to doing more of the things you find most satisfying and important in life. When you have completed your design for an ideal daily round, discuss what this review has meant to you with a close friend, partner or family member or with the other members of this group.

(Adapted from Mark A. Burch's study in *Simplicity* pp.72–74). [20]

OR Begin to read some of the contemplative literature that makes up our rich Christian heritage.
Good people to start with are Thomas à Kempis, Thomas Merton and Henri Nouwen.

Prayer

Be Still and Know

In turmoil rushing round I search for God
The whirlwind in my soul seeks for my Lord
Where can I find him?
Amid the roarings of the wind I am afraid
I cannot hear his voice above the storm
How shall I hear him?
Tossed in the desperation of my mind
I call in terror yearning for his grace
When will I know him?
Then as I stand in desolation, naked and alone,
Silently at the very centre of my soul
The Spirit answers
Be still and know that I am God.

(Anon)

'Next week there can't be any crisis. My schedule is already full.'
Henry Kissinger

Be Still and Know that I am God (Psalm 46 v10)

Here I am, Lord, again, at the place where we meet
And there you are, as ever, quietly waiting on the threshold.
My invitation to you was last-minute and hasty.
Sure of your availability, I sent you no card.
The meal is unprepared, but I open the door and you come in;
You, who of all are most worthy....
Prepared, it would seem, to eat the crumbs from my table.

Careless of my privilege, I have not secured the door
And in behind you steal the gatecrashers,
The cares and concerns of the moment.
They set up a commotion in the room, these uninvited ones.
It's difficult to hear and I can't concentrate.
My attention wanders and I look aside from you, to them.
The hubbub of their conversation fascinates me,
While you, so still and quiet, seem easier to ignore.
Aware that your attention is still with me, and guilty of my lack of hospitality, I offer you the occasional, polite exchange
For, after all, you are my guest.

The intruders have no manners.
Intolerant of each other, they jostle and push, clamouring for attention.
They remind me of my shortcomings of this not done, that not sent.
I feel them closing in.
In the pandemonium of that room, I stumble out and cry out
"O Jesus, Lord of all, have mercy."
You, Lord, the perfect guest, are still there, arms proffered.
I lean..... and slowly ...slowly the noise recedes.
Bored at last from lack of activity the intruders go, closing the door behind them.

All is still now, in that quiet meeting place which is my soul...
And I, your guest now,
Have come at last into that place where all along you had beckoned me.
Within the veil.

I look up, and the bright light of your countenance overwhelms me
Joy... peace... wholeness... I am nothing
I in you
You in me
We are one.

(Glenda Waddell, unpublished)

'Know the true value of time, snatch, seize and enjoy every moment of it.'
Lord Chesterfield

Further Reading and Resources

- Richard Foster, *Celebration of Discipline* (Hodder & Stoughton, 1989). See especially the chapter on solitude.
- Paul Mills, *A Brief Theology of Time*. Part 2: Resisting the Tyranny of Time.
- Michael Schut (ed.), *Simpler Living: Compassionate Life* (Thomas More Press, 1999).
- Tom Sine, *Mustard Seed Vs. McWorld: Reinventing Christian Life for a New Millenium* (Monarch, 1999).

'No-one ever said on their death-bed, "I wish I'd spent more time in the office."'
Rob Parsons

Notes

Notes

SESSION THREE

Neither Poverty nor Riches

'Give me neither poverty nor riches, but give me only my daily bread. Otherwise, I may have too much and disown you and say, "Who is the Lord?" or I may become poor and steal, and so dishonour the name of my God' (Proverbs 30:8–9).

Goals

- To gain an understanding of what the Bible teaches about money and possessions.
- To begin to explore its implications for us today.

Reading

Money certainly seems to make the world go round. Wherever we look and whatever we do we are faced with the belief that our goal, whether as individuals, businesses or nations, is to make more money and to build a 'better' life, surrounding ourselves with the trappings of that wealth.

> 'You and I and the Wilcoxes stand upon money as upon islands. It is so firm beneath our feet that we forget its very existence. Last night when we were talking up here round the fire I began to think that the very soul of the world is economic, and that the lowest abyss is not the absence of love, but the absence of coin.' (E.M. Forster, Howard's End)[21]

So many of the issues involved with living a simpler lifestyle revolve around our understanding of money and possessions. Because of this, three of the sessions in this course will focus on this topic. As Christians we want to be people who are following God's values and not the world's and so our session this week aims to provide a foundational understanding of the Bible's teaching in this area. If we can gain a good grasp of what the Bible says, it will revolutionise the way we approach the rest of the topics in the weeks to come. Next week's materials will build on that, looking more at what that means for us now, and then a later session picks up on some of the broader issues to do with our use of money, considering topics that are not so commonly discussed.

The Bible is the story of God's unfolding plan for humanity, starting with the very Creation of the world. The Creation narrative of Genesis 1 and 2 bursts on us in a wonderful stream of positivity: everything God created was good. There is no repudiation of the material world, but an absolute embracing of it.

The world is created in all its abundance. Its blessings and fullness are there for people to enjoy. Nevertheless, it does not take long for this to be destroyed and the narrative of the Fall depicts humanity's turning away from God and choosing to go their own way. The consequences are played out instantly in the following chapters as we see the introduction of, among other things, relational disharmony (3:16), painful toil in childbearing and work (3: 16, 17–19); greed (4:1–16); and pride (11:1–9).

When the stranger asks the meaning of the city – whether people huddle together because they love one another – will the answer be: 'We all dwell together to make money from each other' or 'This is a community'?
T. S. Eliot

The call of Abram (Genesis 12) starts a new chapter in God's dealings with humanity. He has chosen Abram to be the father of a nation who will carry out God's plans for the rest of the world. They are to be a blessing to the nations around them and, through that, are to be the means by which the whole of the world is brought into a worshipping relationship with him. A central element of the promises that God makes with Abraham (Genesis 17) is that his people will be given the land of Canaan in which to live and prosper as they obey him. The theme of the land richly 'flowing with milk and honey' is a central part of the Exodus story (eg Exodus 3:8) and the rest of the Old Testament is the story of how Israel pursues that calling both to possess and to live in the 'Promised Land'; of her continual failings; and of the never-ending faithfulness of Yahweh, her God.

One of the foundational events in the life of Israel is the Exodus, as God calls a nation into being out of a bedraggled group of slaves. This event is crucial in the shaping of Israel and in informing its people of the way they are to live before God. They start their life as a nation in a situation of poverty: dispossessed and in slavery. They owe their whole being to the God who rescued them; nothing Israel has is their own for everything belongs to Yahweh.

The laws that govern their relationship with God thus reflect this situation. Unlike the other nations around them, they are to be a people who look after the poor and the foreigner, the widow and the dispossessed for such were they when God delivered them. Because everything belongs to God, the laws legislate strongly against inequality (see, for example, the laws against moving boundary stones, Deuteronomy 19:14, 27:17, which also, of course, assume that people had their own private property). The most well-known laws to this effect were those of the Jubilee (Leviticus 25) which legislated that, each fifty years, everyone should return to their own property and clan. It would appear that these laws were never properly followed – at least for long – and thus, as Israel became a monarchy, huge inequalities developed, often at the expense of the poor.

Thus, throughout the Old Testament two strands appear regarding money and possessions. On the one hand, there is nothing intrinsically wrong with having either and, indeed, they are to be seen as part of the promises of Yahweh for those who live according to his ways (but note that Craig Blomberg, among others, is clear that this is one strand of teaching that does not carry through into the New Testament[22]). God is seen as a God of tremendous generosity and blessing: a God who rescued his people out of poverty, rather than calling them into it! Wealth creation is a calling that God can occasionally (if not rarely) give a person and to be denied that ability can be a denial of God's purposes for our lives (for example, the story of Joseph in Genesis 39:2–6, and Proverbs 3:9–10). We have been placed in a world full of plenty and our response should not be to reject that plenty, but rather to accept and manage it effectively.

And yet the other strand is that a person's money or property should never be gained at the expense of another, who is thereby left in a poorer state. The Lausanne paper so clearly states that 'involuntary poverty is an offence against the goodness of God'.[23] The prophets provide us with a strong denunciation of the situation of gross inequality that arose within Israel. Craig Blomberg points to five specific sins of Israel relating to material possessions against which the prophets cry out: worshipping idols made of costly materials (Isaiah 2:7–8); trusting in ritual rather than repentance (Jeremiah 7:4); extorting, robbing and oppressing to gain more land (Ezekiel 22:29); boasting in wealth (Amos 6:4–6) and financial motivation for a leader's ministry (Micah 3:11). In contrast to this, the five things which Israel should do are to seek justice for the marginalised (Isaiah 58:6–7); not boast in riches but be generous in giving them away (Jeremiah 9:23–24); lament one's sins and the horrible consequences they generate (Lamentations); seek the welfare of the city (Jeremiah 29:7) and cling to promises of restoration (Isaiah Chapters 54–55 and 60–66).[24]

Thus, while we do not find an ascetism in the Old Testament that condemns money or possessions in themselves, there are voices, such as those heard in the Laws of the Jubilee, that point clearly to there being limits to wealth. They demonstrate that our understanding of these things should always be within the context of an overriding concern for the poor.

When we turn to look at Jesus we will be disappointed if we hope to find him only concerned with individual piety. The fact that for him giving is as important as praying and fasting (Matthew 6) and that, apart from the kingdom of God, Jesus talks more about money than about anything else, shows how crucial this issue was to him. And, if we are hoping

'There is enough in the world for man's need but not for man's greed.'
Gandhi

for a soft approach from him, we will again be sorely disappointed. Jesus was very clear that we cannot serve both God and Mammon /money (Matthew 6:24) and taught strongly about the dangers of money. He described riches as a strangler (Luke 8:14) and as a worry (Luke 12:22–34). Money can blind us to the eternal realities of life (Luke 16:9–31) and indeed can be a curse for us (Luke 6:20–24).[25]

More positively, Jesus gives the flipside to why we should not be preoccupied with money: because we should seek first the kingdom of God (Matthew 6:33), as we saw in Session One. Jesus challenges head-on our society's obsession with material things (our 'treasures') and instead puts before us the values of the kingdom (Matthew 6:19–34).[26] The gauntlet is thrown down: what do we put our security in? Is it in God's provision or in our material possessions? Which are more important to us? What are we investing in for the long-term? Do we have an eternal perspective when we consider these things? How important are clothes and food to us? Do we 'run after these things' rather than after the kingdom of God?

Jesus' message of radical kingdom economics is summed up in two incidents in his life. Firstly, in Luke 19, Zacchaeus shows us a person who, before meeting Jesus, put all his trust and value in his wealth. Martin Luther once said that 'every person needs two conversions: one of the heart and one of the wallet'. Here we see a person demonstrating those two conversions working together. Zacchaeus' money was made at the expense of the poor people of Jericho and he knew that the only appropriate response on meeting Jesus was to give back all that money – and not just to give it back, but return it fourfold!

As he gave away half of his possessions to the poor and then paid people back four times over, we can only guess at the financial effect that had on him. It is unlikely that he would have been rich after that. There was no giving away of his surplus to make himself feel better. This was a radical outworking of the Jubilee principle.

The second incident in Jesus' life was his observation of the widow giving her two very small coins (Luke 21). In contrast to all the wealthy people who were also putting their gifts into the temple treasury, Jesus recognises that 'this poor widow has put in more than all the others'. Again we see how different the values of the kingdom are from the values of society. In our world, size and numbers count: we are praised for the amount we give. In Jesus' eyes what matters is how much we have left afterwards and the sacrifice that we have been prepared to make.

The early church continued Jesus' economic ethic, as the early chapters of Acts bear out. What is envisaged here is not necessarily communal living with private ownership of property prohibited – clearly people throughout the early church owned their own houses and fields – but a radical community where most things were held in common, and where members were prepared to give abundantly of their own possessions and money in order to see that others' needs were met.

Hengel says that:

> Primitive Christianity contains a radical criticism of riches, a demand for detachment from the goods of this world and a conquest of the barriers between the rich and poor through the fellowship of agape. All this comes about under the shadow of the imminent coming of the Kingdom of God. It robs unrighteous mammon of its force.[27]

The call was to share God's blessings with his followers but also not to neglect the poor with whom they came into contact.

Paul uses the collection for the church in Jerusalem as an opportunity to demonstrate that the Christian's attitude towards, and use of, money is not a peripheral issue (2 Corinthians 8:1–15). In his letters we get a glimpse of the early church reaching more into the middle and upper classes. In particular, the church at Corinth ran into problems through people expecting to be able to use their wealth to buy power within the church and Paul again sets out the contrast between Jesus' way and the world's way.

'One way is to accumulate more. The other way is to desire less'.
G. K. Chesterton

James more famously picks this up and his words contain a strong challenge for us today: do we treat people differently according to their financial status? (James 2:1–5). How does our faith manifest itself? Do we see someone who is in need and wish them well without helping them or are we prepared to accompany our faith by action? His words provide a fitting conclusion to our look at what the Bible says about money and possessions:

> What good is it if a person claims to have faith but has no deeds? Can such faith save him? Suppose a brother or sister is without clothes and daily food. If one of you says to them, "Go, I wish you well; keep warm and well fed", but does nothing about their physical needs, what good is it? In the same way, faith by itself, if it is not accompanied by action, is dead. (James 2:14–17)

Discussion

'Last night was a real impactful evening for me and the others who attended. The Spirit was truly at work, and I appreciated the openness and intimacy with which we talked about our money and giving.'

- Look together at the Jubilee laws (Leviticus 25) and discuss their implications. What effects would they have had on the nation of Israel?
- In the reading we saw that the Old Testament teaches that a person's money or property should never be gained at the expense of another. How does that apply to us today, both individually and corporately? Is it too late to do anything about it? What challenges does the story of Zacchaeus (Luke 19) present to us?
- What do you think Jesus' view of simplicity is?
- In your own words what was the central message of Jesus' economic teaching?
- What, if any, constraints do you think there should be today on the accumulation and retention of money and possessions?
- In what ways are we not acting on the Bible's teaching? What stops us? Fear? Indifference? Introspection? Inertia? Incompetence?
- Do we treat people differently in our church according to their financial status?

Action and Homework

Use this week to pray through what the Bible teaches about money and possessions and ask God to speak to you about one particular area in your life that needs changing in this regard. Allow God to begin changing you through his Holy Spirit – remember, we cannot do anything ourselves, but have to allow God to work in us.

Further Reading and Resources

- Craig Blomberg, *Neither Poverty Nor Riches: a Biblical Theology of Possessions* (IVP, 2001).
- Donald Kraybill, *The Upside-down Kingdom* (Herald Press, 1991).
- Keith Tondeur, *What Jesus Said About Money and Possessions* (Monarch Books, 1998).
- Ron Sider, *Rich Christians in An Age of Hunger* (Hodder & Stoughton 1998).

'If any one of you has material possessions and sees a brother or sister in need but has no pity on them, how can the love of God be in you?'
1 John 3:17

Notes

Notes

SESSION FOUR

Money and Wealth

'For the love of money is a root of all kinds of evil. Some people, eager for money, have wandered from the faith and pierced themselves with many griefs' (1 Timothy 6:10).

'Get up early, work hard, strike oil.' John Paul Getty on how to get wealthy.

Goals

- To understand the meaning of stewardship.
- To examine our own ability to steward money and wealth.
- To reflect on the role that money plays in our lives.

Reading

Having looked last week at the Bible's teaching on money and possessions, this week we continue our discussion on what that means for us now: how we can both have and use our money today. This is often talked about in terms of stewardship.

Stewardship

Stewardship is central to any and every discussion about money and possessions. The extent to which it is understood by a community of believers is the corresponding extent to which it will transform the lives of all of those within that community. Nothing that we have belongs to us (Psalm 24:1): we hold it all in trust for God to do with as he pleases. This is the real principle of stewardship. Whatever we have, we have either acquired it as a result of the gifts and talents which God has given to us or we have received it unearned by us as a gift or by way of inheritance.

Either way, as John Wesley writes in his 1768 sermon, The Good Steward:

> '[The steward] is not the proprietor of anything which is in his hands but [is] barely entrusted with them by another.........We are not at liberty to use what [God] has lodged in our hands as we please but as he pleases.'

Yet most of us spend a lot of our time comparing what we have to what others around us have and either coveting what someone else has or bemoaning what we lack and the peer pressure can be considerable – both outside and inside the church. Furthermore there is a strong desire in all of us to ensure that those to whom we are close have the best we can afford to give them.'

Trust

To be faithful stewards we are called to trust God that he will provide for all of our needs. That is the thrust of the passage in the Sermon on the Mount (Matthew 6:25–34): 'Therefore I tell you, do not worry about your life, what you will eat or drink; or about your body, what you will wear. Is not life more important than food and the body more important than clothes?'

'No-one can be a slave to two masters. Either you will hate the one and love the other, or you will be devoted to the one and despise the other. You cannot be a slave to both God and money'
Matthew 6:24

Most of us, when reading that passage, want to put in a reality check straight away and we say, 'Well yes, but God can't mean it just like that. We can't be wholly dependent on him in that way, can we?' It is true that, in the ordinary course of events, God will not expect to put food on our table if we have not lifted a finger to earn the money to buy that food. So far as it is within our power we are called upon to use our gifts and talents so that we are not dependent on others (1 Thessalonians 4:11–12) and to make appropriate family provision for those who are rightly dependent upon us (1 Timothy 5:8). But the main point is that we can and should trust him and not be anxious about where tomorrow's food is coming from. Once we learn how to do this, what a sense of freedom that brings! How wonderful truly to be able to concentrate on the kingdom of God and not on all these other things.

The trouble so often is that we are rarely in a position where we must trust his complete provision for us, and yet the Bible is full of examples of both natural and supernatural provision. In the West we have in large part lost the culture of trusting God. Both individually and as a church many of us have been taken in by the world.

The Extent of our Stewardship

As with any good steward, God requires that we know exactly what it is that he has granted us to keep in trust at any given time. How many of us know exactly how much money we have, what we spend, what we save and what we give away? This needs to be a first priority in using our money for God.

Needs

Knowing what it is that we have stewardship over we can then begin to work out what to do with it, starting with our needs. If we are only stewards of all we possess we should be wary of using any of it for ourselves without consulting God – and thus a clear and biblical approach to our needs is unavoidable. We have to develop our understanding of needs not just in the context of the poor but in order to address our lifestyle choices correctly.

Some of us reading this material might be struggling to survive. Poverty in the UK is a reality. Some 13 million people are living on a low income and 85,000 families are in temporary accommodation.[28] For most of us, the right comparison is not necessarily with others in our society but with the three billion people on this planet who live in abject poverty or worse.

The idea of need is almost always relative. The temptation is to compare ourselves with our neighbours down the road when it comes to needs but it is neither biblical nor honest to do so. When we look 'up the ladder' we are never rich and always need more, but the Jubilee perspective tells us to 'look down' and then we are always rich and suddenly our 'needs' seem to disappear.[29] That said, different people will have different perceptions of need in any given area and the discussion is rarely simple.

Everything is Possible

Let us look at an example of Jesus' attitude towards money and wealth:

> As Jesus started on his way, a man ran up to him and fell on his knees, before him. 'Good teacher,' he asked, 'what must I do to inherit eternal life?' 'Why do you call me good?' Jesus answered. 'No one is good – except God alone. You know the commandments: "Do not murder, do not commit adultery, do not steal, do not give false testimony, do not defraud, honour your father and mother."' 'Teacher', he declared, 'all these I have kept since I was a boy.'
>
> Jesus looked at him and loved him. 'One thing you lack,' he said. 'Go, sell everything you have and give to the poor, and you will have treasure in heaven. Then come, follow me.' At this the man's face fell. He went away sad, because he had great wealth.

'Covetousness we call ambition
Hoarding we call prudence
Greed we call industry.'
Anon

> Jesus looked around and said to his disciples, 'How hard it is for the rich to enter the kingdom of God!' The disciples were amazed at his words. But Jesus said again, 'Children, how hard it is to enter the kingdom of God! It is easier for a camel to go through the eye of a needle than for a rich person to enter the kingdom of God.' The disciples were even more amazed, and said to one another, 'Who then can be saved?' Jesus looked at them and said, 'With people this is impossible, but not with God; all things are possible with God'. (Mark 10:17–31).

Jesus' reaction to the question, 'Good teacher, what must I do to inherit eternal life?' is surprising – he resists the flattery and points straight to God. 'No-one is good – except God alone.' Then Jesus reels off a list of commandments which the young man says he has kept since he was a boy. Note that Jesus does not mention the greatest ones of 'love the Lord your God with all your heart and with all your soul and with all your mind and love your neighbour as yourself' (Matthew 22:37–39).

Verse 21 describes a breathtaking scene. 'Jesus looked at him and loved him'. Imagine knowing that the eyes of the Lord are loving you. What could that man have felt like to have Jesus love him like that? But then he says, in the context of that great love, 'One thing you lack. Go, sell everything you have and give to the poor, and you will have treasure in heaven. Then come, follow me.'

One thing you lack – for this man, as for so many of us, there was one thing which held him back from being in relationship with Jesus Christ: his money and wealth. 'At this the man's face fell. He went away sad, because he had great wealth.' Is it possible to come face to face with our Lord and Saviour Jesus Christ and yet to go away sad?
The Bible is full of wonderful stories of how women, men and children came to Jesus and were healed or filled with the Holy Spirit or simply loved and went away rejoicing and praising God. Yet, this man experienced the deep love of God and still went away sad because of his love for money!

John Wesley writes in one of his sermons when he speaks about God and money:

> Does not every man see that he cannot comfortably serve both? That to trim between God and the world is the sure way to be disappointed in both, and to have no rest either in one or the other? How uncomfortable a condition must he be in who, having the fear, but not the love of God, who, serving him, but not with all his heart, has only the toils and not the joys of religion? He has religion enough to make him miserable, but not enough to make him happy: his religion will not let him enjoy the world; and the world will not let him enjoy God. So that by halting between both, he loses both; and has no peace either in God or in the world. [30]

That man was torn between a world promising apparent security, endless pleasure and comfort and Jesus' call to give up everything and follow him. For the rich young man it was the end of the story, but we can hear it in full.

Jesus clearly states in verse 23: 'How hard it is for the rich to enter the kingdom of God!' and then says it again: 'Children, how hard it is to enter the kingdom of God! It is easier for a camel to go through the eye of a needle than for a rich person to enter the kingdom of God.' But then Jesus said, 'With people this is impossible'. It is hard to give up wealth and money in our own strength mainly because we don't want to. We don't even want to want to give them up! 'But not with God; all things are possible with God.' If that young man had stayed just a little longer he would have heard these vital and soothing words:

> 'I tell you the truth, no one who has left home or brothers or sisters or mother or father or children or fields for me and the gospel will fail to receive a hundred times as much in this present age (homes, brothers, sisters, mothers, children and fields – and with them, persecutions) and in the age to come, eternal life. But many who are first will be last and the last will be first' (Mark 10:29–31).

'With people this is impossible, but not with God; all things are possible with God.'

'If you live for having it all, what you have is never enough. In an environment of more is better. 'Enough' is like the horizon, always receding. You lose the ability to identify that point of sufficiency at which you can choose to stop.'
Joe Dominguez and Vicki Robin, Your Money or Your Life

Jesus' offer was to become part of a loving community where there was more than enough for everyone, where the rich young ruler could learn how to love and love deeply by being loved and loved deeply. How unequal an offer this was if all that the young man could bring to that community was money.

Discussion

- Read together the story of the rich young ruler (Mark 10:17–31). What was Jesus' offer to him?
- What is your understanding of stewardship?
- How would you feel about disclosing your annual income and the capital you have available to those with whom you pray or to this group? Why is it difficult to do? Should we be more transparent? Should we ensure that we are accountable for our income and expenditure choices and for our use of capital?
- Do you know people or families whose use of money you respect? Tell the group about them.[31]
- Why is it hard to trust God to supply all your needs?
- What would your life be like if your income was suddenly halved? What changes would you have to make?
- Can you imagine living with less money?
- How much is enough?

In your discussion time think of some ways in which you could honour God more with your money.

'This chapter and the previous one spoke very powerfully to me in an issue I had been dealing with at work. In essence, the Lord provides for all our needs yet I wanted to badger bosses for more money rather than go and ask my heavenly father. I was then prompted to remember [a man] who prayerfully takes his financial needs to the Lord, who in turn has covered them, rather than go and ask friends for more money. Once this light was switched on I was then able to recognise I have more than enough, and should I need more I will go to the Lord and ask him first.'

Some Examples:

Impose on yourself a luxury tax. Whenever you buy something for yourself that is a luxury, like a bar of chocolate, a cinema ticket or a car (!) buy two and give one away. (From a talk by Phil Wall – then in the Salvation Army.)

OR every month put aside a sum of money (it could be as little as 50p) and when you have a fair amount give it away or buy something for someone.

OR as a group start a fund which you contribute to regularly over and above your regular giving to the church (discipline is important) and again give it away as and when you feel it appropriate.

OR give regularly and in a tax-efficient manner to a charity which you know and trust.

OR look at setting yourself a fixed maximum rate of income.

OR consider together the concept of the graduated tithe as put forward by Ron Sider in *Rich Christians in an Age of Hunger* (pp.193–196). Ask yourself, how would you want to adapt it if you chose to use it in your life?

'The inward reality of simplicity involves a life of joyful unconcern for possessions. Neither the greedy nor the miserly know that liberty. It has nothing to do with abundance or possession or lack. It is an inward spirit of trust.'
Richard Foster, Celebration of Discipline

Homework

J. Edgar Hoover (!) said, 'A budget tells your money where to go, otherwise you wonder where it went!' If you do not already have a personal budgeting system, try using the 'Looking after your Personal Money' in Appendix 3. It has been prepared as part of the training and preparation of those who are to set up their own businesses with assistance from FACE to Face.

'Personal Money was a breakthrough area in my life. Hope I've formed a habit. I'm still doing it and still saving my £2.'

Draw up for yourself an account of what you spent your income on over the past year. Try to account for as much as possible, including major purchases in the past twelve months – if you do not have a good record system go through your bank statements and cheque stubs. Go to the budgeting system in the appendix for help on this. Then ask yourself:

1. Am I happy with where my income came from?
2. Does my financial life function separately from the rest of my life?
3. Have I spent more than I received? If so what immediate changes are necessary in my expenditure choices so that I can live within my income?
4. Does what I spend my money on please God?
5. Does what I spend my money on help me to be active in my community (for example, sport) or do I spend it in a way which keeps me isolated (for example, watching TV or playing computer games)?
6. How tied am I to my regular debt repayments and instalment payments?
   What changes can I make (a) to leave behind past choices which I am still paying for and (b) so that I live only within my current income and savings?
7. Do I save up for expensive items or do I buy them on credit? Am I happy with this method of shopping?
8. Do I need to make changes to my lifestyle to facilitate some of the above?

Now make a budgeting plan that would allow you to live on 90% of your present income or make only 90% of your present expenditures, reducing to 80% after three months and 50% after six months. What changes would you have to make? Try to devise a workable plan and think about the shifts in lifestyle that would be required. Consider both the disadvantages and advantages of such changes. What would you gain? What would you lose? What would be the opportunities in such a situation? Which, if any, of these changes are you going to make?[32]

Prayer

Consider how to get into the habit of praying through all financial decisions, small and large.

'I have never been so on top of my finances, ever.'

Further Reading and Resources

- Keith Tondeur, *Your Money and Your Life* (Penguin, 1999).
- Keith Tondeur, *Financial Tips for the Family: an Essential Guide* (Hodder & Stoughton, 1997).

  Good for the first steps in learning how to manage money in your family.
- Michael Schut (ed.), *Simpler Living: Compassionate Life* (Thomas More Press, 1999).

  See among others the excellent article by Alan Durning, How Much is Enough? pp.90–99.
- Ron Sider, *Rich Christians in an Age of Hunger* (Hodder & Stoughton 1998).

'Keep your lives free from the love of money and be content with what you have, because God has said, "Never will I leave you; never will I forsake you". So we say with confidence, "The Lord is my helper, I will not be afraid. What can people do to me?"'
Hebrews 13:5–6

Notes

Notes

SESSION FIVE

Consumerism[33]

'All the believers were one in heart and mind. No one claimed that any of their possessions were their own, but they shared everything they had. With great power the apostles continued to testify to the resurrection of the Lord Jesus, and much grace was upon them all. There were no needy persons among them. For from time to time those who owned land or houses sold them, brought the money from the sales and put it at the apostles' feet, and it was distributed to anyone as they had need. Joseph, a Levite from Cyprus, whom the apostles called Barnabas (which means Son of Encouragement), sold a field he owned and brought the money and put it at the apostles' feet' (Acts 4:32–37).

Goals

- To understand when possessions add satisfaction to our lives and when they distract us from what is important.
- To understand the culture we are living in and the effect it has on our faith.
- To explore why we want so many things.

Reading

After the war there was an era of mass consumption on an unprecedented scale. A productivity boom enabled goods and services to be supplied in a capacity which far outstripped demand. The only way to deal with this volume was to stimulate demand. In other words, to produce a desire to consume. This led to all the marketing ploys with which we are now so familiar: advertising, built-in obsolescence, the promotion of credit cards and the creation of new areas of consumption such as the teen and yuppy markets.

The result is that consumerism is now the dominant force in our society. The worth or significance of people is now defined by what they consume – house, car, holiday, clothes, electrical equipment or whatever else is on offer. The advertisements surrounding us make sure we can distinguish between a Volvo and a Renault Clio driver and can identify a Hamlet smoker or a Bacardi drinker. As community and family identity have increasingly been eroded, so finding our identity in our possessions has become the norm. Our possessions have possessed us. How swiftly we have moved from 'How do you do?' to 'What do you do?'

As identity is now primarily found in what we consume, so people often build their supporting communities around their consumption habits. If you don't believe that, think about your family and friends. Ask yourself to what extent your bonding with them is done around the things you consume – things like dinner out or a shopping trip. How much of your conversation is about activities or objects of consumption?

Because of this, consumerism is, at its heart, self-centred and individualistic. This unites it closely to its partner, post-modernity, which focuses on the autonomy of the individual and the 'rights' of individuals to whatever they want.

'We buy things we do not want to impress people we do not like.'
(Anon)

As our television sets become inundated with 'Watchdog' programmes which look at the rights of the consumer to stand up against shoddy goods, one cannot help but wish that the consumer would demonstrate equal passion over issues of fair trade and the environmental consequences of consumption (that is, the rights of the producer). Standing over all of this is the power of money. Money is all-important because without it one cannot consume. It is endlessly presented as the bringer of status, power and freedom, and hence that elusive prize: happiness.

As followers of Jesus we know a different story. We know that we do not need to be surrounded by 'stuff' in order to find fulfilment. We can experience the freedom that Paul expresses in Philippians 4:12–13:

> I have learned the secret of being content in any and every situation, whether well fed or hungry, whether living in plenty or in want. I can do everything through him who gives me strength.

As we simplify our lives and refuse to be shackled by the chains of consumerism, so we shall discover a new sense of joy and liberation.

The bigger picture of consumerism is seen in its global effect. There are many causes of poverty which include sinful personal choices, natural disasters, lack of technology and past western colonialism. But we must recognise that the cult of consumerism is a part of the pernicious structures that contribute to world poverty. Whether it is through market economies, issues of trade, debt or the environment, the goods we buy here are directly linked to the lives of others throughout the world. As Christians we have a responsibility to be aware of how our actions affect other people and to do all we can to help. The writer of Proverbs says that *'the righteous care about justice for the poor, but the wicked have no such concern'* (Proverbs 29:7).

Consider:

> 'Having does not define being, as ten seconds of introspection reveals. But market economies teach us to associate the consumption of goods and services closely with non-material states of consciousness and feelings that do define being. It takes a considerable act of self-awareness to disentangle the two. The result is that the idea of having less, no matter how just the cause, feels to us like being less.' (Mark A. Burch, *Simplicity*, p.27)

> 'Our enormously productive economy... demands that we make consumption our way of life, that we convert the buying and use of goods into rituals, that we seek our spiritual satisfaction, our ego satisfaction, in consumption... We need things consumed, burned up, worn out, replaced and discarded at an ever increasing rate.' Victor Lebow in the Journal of Retailing (mid-50s) (From Mark A. Burch, *Simplicity*, p.13)

> 'According to Schor [who conducted a lengthy survey of employees at a telecommunications company in America], the really, really surprising variable was education. Conventional wisdom says that more educated people will be more educated consumers. Instead she found the reverse. The greater the level of education, she found, the higher the level of spending. Better educated people were more tied to the culture of upscale consuming. Education raised aspirations.' (Enough! Fall 1998)

> 'We find advertising works the way grass grows. You can never see it, but every week you have to mow the lawn.' (Andy Tarshis, quoted in Robert Heath, *The Hidden Power of Advertising*.)

> 'Bargain: something you can't use at a price you can't resist.' (Franklin P. Jones.)

> 'One major consequence of brand decisions being made by intuition is that consumers often have little explicit memory of exactly what it was that made them choose the brand...Why do we believe we are immune to emotional advertising, when it is evident from the success of campaigns, that we are in many ways defenceless suckers?'
> (Robert Heath, *The Hidden Power of Advertising*.)

'Once I seriously began to confront issues of poverty and justice, I had no spiritual or ethical alternative but to change radically my pattern of living. I was forced to reshape my choices: what I ate, what I bought, how I travelled and the neighbourhoods I lived in.'
'A Spirituality of Contentment', Dee Dee Risher from The Other Side, Northwest Earth Institute, 1992

Regardless of what advertising tells us, our real hunger is not for things but for a better image of ourselves, either in the eyes of others or in our own eyes. This can only be found in Jesus Christ. No amount of material possessions can ever make us secure or fulfilled.

There is almost no end to the list of things that we consume. However, here are a few of the most common ones illustrated by quotes and statistics. The reason for reading them is to make us think and to enable us to discuss difficult issues both in the context of our own home as well as in the world as a whole. Don't be put off if it all seems rather overwhelming. As has been stressed before, we are all at different stages and will differ as to how much we are able to take these things on board. These are momentous issues and the idea is that you whet your appetite rather than attempt to cover everything in one session.

Food

'Most urban dwellers are unaware that eating is an agricultural act. They no longer know or imagine the connection between eating and the land. They mostly ignore critical questions about their food. How fresh is it? Was it grown with or without dangerous chemicals? How far was it transported? How did processing affect its nutritional value? This has happened because of the industrialisation of farming, extensive processing of food, and the fast pace of life. A wall has been erected that separates the eater from the source of his food. ... one would not know that the various edibles were ever living creatures, or that they come from the soil, or that they were produced by work.'
(*Voluntary Simplicity* (Northwest Earth Institute) pp.VII–5.)

'There is a politics of food that, like any politics, involves our freedom. We still (sometimes) remember that we cannot be free if our minds and voices are controlled by someone else. But we have neglected to understand that we cannot be free if our food and its sources are controlled by someone else. The condition of the passive consumer of food is not a democratic condition. One reason to eat responsibly is to eat free.'
(Wendell Berry, "The Pleasures of Eating", in: Michael Schut (ed.), *Simpler Living:Compassionate Life*, p.106.)

'Food distribution by road freight is now the fastest growing transport sector in the UK and is a major contributor to air pollution. Twelve per cent of the nation's fuel consumption is spent on transporting and packaging food. The same amount of food is travelling 50% further around the country than fifteen years ago. The UK exports 12m tonnes of food and drink and imports 20m tonnes – a ridiculous swap.'
(The Soil Association, *Local Food for Local People*, 1998)

Television and Advertising

'Whilst our advertising-soaked culture makes it difficult for anyone to reject consumerism, it's foolish to claim that it has been forced on people. If anything, people seem to love consumerism. They actively choose to embrace it.'
(Enough! Website)

'According to a recent poll, one in four young Britons would rather give up their partner than part with their television set. The poll on leisure activities and spending also said that the majority of people in Britain ranked their TV as their most prized possession.' (Enough! Spring 1999)

'Television advertising takes exceedingly trivial concerns (such as which deodorant, shampoo, or denture adhesive to use) and blows them up into issues of seemingly enormous importance for our lives. Concerns that are utterly insignificant relative to the task of making it through this time of profound ecological and social transition are given vastly inflated significance and then force-fed into our collective consciousness. To break the cultural hypnosis of consumerism, we must begin by breaking the corporate stranglehold on television.'
(Duane Elgin, *Voluntary Simplicity*, p.203)

'We have come to believe, deeply, that it is our right to consume. If we have the money, we can buy whatever we want, whether or not we need it, use it or even enjoy it... Born to shop. Whoever dies with the most toys wins. Life, liberty and the pursuit of material possessions.'
Joe Dominguez and Vicki Robin, Your Money or Your Life

Fashion

'Clothing is inseparable from identity. In a society which is losing its grasp on heroism in terms of faith and values, the street heroism each one of us can indulge in is fashion. Our appearance can startle, stun, excite, cause admiration and emulation.' (Mike Starkey, *Born to Shop*, p.55)

'The UK beauty industry takes £8.9 billion a year from women.' (Germaine Greer, *The Whole Woman*, p.23)

'Woman... is the emblem of spending ability and the chief spender, she is also the most effective seller of this world's goods. Every survey ever held has shown that the image of an attractive woman is the most effective advertising gimmick.' (Germaine Greer, *The Female Eunuch*, p.60)

'What the glossies are good at is the stimulation of desire for what we haven't got and the creation of anxiety about our own attributes; they wish us to believe that our aspirations are attainable with a little judicious remodelling and investment in the kinds of commodities advertised within their pages.'
(Imelda Whelehan, *Overloaded: Popular Culture and the Future of Feminism*, p.138)

'I'd kill myself if I was that fat.' (Liz Hurley on Marilyn Monroe)

'Refuse to keep up with clothing fashions. Very few readers of this book need to buy clothes – except perhaps shoes – for two or three years.' (Ron Sider, *Rich Christians in an Age of Hunger*, p.200)

Holidays

'Strange as it may seem, the majority of our holidays are part of a vast industry. In fact, tourism is the biggest industry in the world.[35] There were 693 million 'tourist arrivals' in 2001 with tourists spending $463 billion around the world.[36] In the UK alone, over 36 million overseas holidays were taken in 2002 (21 million of which were package holidays) and ABTA recorded a combined turnover of £36 billion.'[37]
(R. Valerio, *L is for Lifestyle: Christian Living that Doesn't Cost the Earth*)

'While there is no question that it provides employment in many poor countries, hopes that the industry would provide a progressive alternative to cash-crop economies have not been realised. Local communities may not see much of the income, as tourists often use multinational hotel chains. The Thai Tourist Authority estimates that only 40% of foreign tourist money stays in the country. Many tour operators either take tourists to destinations in oppressive regimes, or have subsidiaries in these countries. In both cases they are giving credence and much needed finance to governments guilty of human rights abuses.' (World Development Movement, *The Good Life*, 1998)

Sport

'The amount we spend on golf every year, estimated at between £20 and £30bn, is the same as the estimated annual cost of providing adequate health care, education, nutrition and clean drinking water to every human being on earth.' (UNICEF, *The State of the World's Children*, 1995)

'The commercialisation of sport is a subtle twisting of sport away from relationships, health, leisure and keen amateurism, towards the cash register.' (Mike Starkey, *Born to Shop*, p.124)

'We're the quirky civilisation that rides elevators to the second floor and buys electronic stair-steppers to condition our thighs. We drive to convenience stores and hurry back to our treadmills. We rely on machines to save us from working, then buy other machines to save our bodies from the terminal flab.' (Business Week)

'The excessive focus on the immediate, the here and now, has created in our society a blindness to the history of how things came to be, and to the legacy this generation will bequeath to the next. The focus on immediate gratification and consumption has created a selfish generation, which has rewarded "buy now, let others pay later" decisions by its political and business leaders.'
Michael Bates

Cars

'About one billion people do most of their travelling on foot. Many in the walking class never go more than 100 miles from their birthplaces. Unable to get to work easily, attend school, or bring their complaints before government offices, they are severely hindered by the lack of transportation options.

'The massive middle class of the world, numbering some three billion people, travels by bus and bicycle. Mile for mile, bikes are cheaper than any other vehicle, costing under $100 in most of the Third World and requiring no fuel. They are also the most efficient form of transportation ever invented and, where not endangered by polluted air and traffic, provide their riders with healthy exercise.

'The world's automobile class is relatively small: only 8% of humans, about 400 million, own cars. The auto class's fleet of four-wheelers is directly responsible for an estimated 13% of carbon dioxide emissions from fossil fuels worldwide, along with air pollution and acid rain, traffic fatalities numbering a quarter million annually, and the sprawl of urban areas into endless tract developments lacking community cohesion.'
(Alan Durning, "How Much is Enough?", in *Simpler Living*, p.93)

'The USA now has more registered vehicles than licensed drivers.'
(Enough! Spring 1999)

Discussion

Do not be phased by the sheer extent of the issues raised by this section. The following may be useful starting points for a discussion about consumerism but the key is likely to be to pick a small number of areas to focus on first, work through them and decide what action to take and then take on another set of issues to think through. No-one should feel that they must change everything all at once – rather, the Almighty will provide a sense of the right priorities for consideration and action.

- Read Hebrews 13:5, Philippians 4:11–12 and 1 Timothy 6:6–10.
  In what ways do these verses speak into our own situations and how can we develop contentment in our lives?
- To what extent do you buy things in order to feel good, to feel secure, to feel different or to make a statement?
- How tied are you to your present job and lifestyle, to instalment payments, maintenance and repair costs, and the expectations of others?
- Do you consider the impact your consumption makes on other people and on the earth?
- Who benefits most from TV? Who suffers?
- What does Christmas mean to you? Do your Christmas activities reflect the values of Jesus or the values of consumerism?
  What could you do differently this year?

'...challenging...relevant... very thought-provoking and topical. The materials really made the group members think and take a step back. Many people's lives have been dramatically altered and they are beginning to think about these issues seriously for the first time.. I think they are a wonderful tool and I would encourage many to do them.'

'When will we admit that the alleviation of world poverty cannot be achieved without sacrifices on the part of the rich?'
Helen Parry, LICC

Action

Consider trying one or some of the following:

- Try not buying food which has already been prepared or chopped or washed. Try not going out for a meal. Spend time thinking about what you are eating.
- Try not watching television for a week/month/year. Then ask yourself the following questions:

  How did I feel about it? Did I miss it? What happened instead?
- Apply the Philippians 4 rule to your TV and cinema viewing: 'Whatever is true, whatever is noble, whatever is right, whatever is pure, whatever is lovely, whatever is admirable – if anything is excellent or praiseworthy – think about such things.' If anything does not fit into this category, ask yourself if it is appropriate to keep watching.
- Try to live without a car for a time (or with only one if you currently have two). How did it affect your life – positively and negatively?
- Look at your holidays – how many do you have each year and how much do you spend on them? Consider not going away this year and giving that amount of money to families you know of who are rarely able to go on holiday.
- Follow the 10% rule. Make an effort to buy 10% fewer packaged goods, 10% fewer processed goods and 10% fewer total goods.
- Go through your wardrobe / kitchen cupboards / whole house (!). Ask yourself, `What do I need? What can I give away?' Then do it! How did it feel? ('Only keep what is useful or what you consider beautiful' – William Morris.)
- Follow the three-month rule. Sort through your kitchen cupboards / whole house (!) and box up anything you don't need/use. If after three months you have not opened the box at all then give it away without opening it .
- Try buying no new clothes for one/three/six/twelve months. Did this cause difficulty?
- Consider the issue of second homes in rural areas. What are the advantages and disadvantages to the local community?
- Limit the use of your car by combining tasks.

Homework

Take these questions with you next time you go shopping (one helpful idea is to make these questions into a credit card!):

- Do I really need this product? Why?
- Is this an impulsive purchase or have I planned it?
- Have I done research to find the best product to meet my needs?
- Do I know the environmental consequences of this purchase?
- Does this product meet fair trade standards?
- Have I considered other alternatives?
- Can I borrow it? Can I barter for it? Can I rent it?
- Can I share it with someone? Can I buy it second hand?
- Was it made or grown locally, perhaps saving energy and packing?

'Often all the possessions we have... are manic attempts to fill this opening [of the soul], but they never stay in place. They always slip, and we are left more vulnerable and exposed than before.'
John O'Donohue, Anam Cara

Further questions:

- Is it reusable/recyclable?
- Is it on sale?
- How will I dispose of it?
- What sort of packaging does it have?
- Is it repairable?
- Can I save on price and packaging by buying in bulk?
- Is it functional?
- Can I buy it from a business which is protecting the environment or human rights?
- How often will I use it?
- If it is clothing, is it comfortable? Will I wear it out before it goes out of fashion?
- Is it healthy for my family and me?
- Does its image convey values I believe in?
- What is the impact of my choice on the environment?
- Do I really need it?

Further Reading and Resources

- John Benton, *Christians in a Consumer Culture* (Christian Focus Publications, 1999).
- Mike Starkey, *Born to Shop* (Monarch Books, 1989).
- Janet Luhrs, *The Simple Living Guide* (Broadway Books, 1997).
- Tom Sine, *Mustard Seed Vs. McWorld: Reinventing Christian Life for a New Millenium* (Monarch Books, 1995).
- The Ethical Consumer: www.ethicalconsumer.org
- World Development Movement, The Good Life, 1998. Available from WDM: www.wdm.org.uk.
- Local organic produce from suppliers such as farmers' markets and box schemes are often cheaper than 'regular' produce from supermarkets. For information on what is available in your area contact the Soil Association: www.soilassocation.org

'The group feel we have developed a pretty deep level of intimacy and openness with each other. People are in action in some way, and are being challenged by the material. So the Spirit is working his stuff.'

'Technology and material things can never liberate you. They have a tendency to squeeze you into their own image.'
Bishop Festo Kivenere, Uganda

Notes

Notes

SESSION SIX

Work

'Whatever you do, work at it with all your heart, as working for the Lord, not for people, since you know that you will receive an inheritance from the Lord as a reward – it is the Lord Christ you are serving. (Colossians 3: 23–24).

Goals

- To evaluate whether work and its related activities are aligned with our purpose and values.
- To understand the biblical values behind work.
- To examine the balance between the need to make a living and the desire for a simple life.

Reading

Do you leap out of bed on a Monday morning, thrilled to be able to start another week's paid work, and do you come home on a Friday night, despondent because the week is over? Perhaps not! There is a need to reappraise how we think about work as Christians and how work is modelled from within the Christ-centred community. It will come as no surprise to hear again that all of us in that community are engaged in full-time service for Jesus all the time. If not, and to the extent that we are not, we are serving either ourselves or the enemy.

Fundamentally, God is a worker. Genesis 2:2, Colossians 1:16–17, Deuteronomy 11:1–7 and John 4:34 give an idea of some of the many things that he does and Psalm 111:2 describes all his works as 'good'. God has created us also to be workers. Ecclesiastes 3:13 and 5:18,19 describe work as a gift from God, an activity of great dignity and significance. Work is thus an important aspect of our self-fulfilment as people, rather than something to be avoided at all costs![38] Not only has he created people to be workers, but he has created us to be co-workers with him. 1 Corinthians 3:5–9, Genesis 2:8–15 and Psalm 8 paint for us a wonderful picture of the model of partnership that God envisages having with us.

Now let us look at what work means for us today. Consider some of these reasons for paid employment and ask yourself which ones apply to you: tradition, enjoyment, duty, prestige, status, power, personal growth, success, creativity, fulfilment, earning money, gaining a sense of security, learning, socialising, structuring time. Have you noticed that work has two different functions: the financial function and the personal function? In reality, there is only one purpose served by paid employment and not by unpaid employment - and that is earning money. The other 'purposes' of paid employment are other types of rewards which are not directly related to getting paid and are all equally available in unpaid activities.[39]

Perhaps this is the most important thing we can learn: that 'work' is not the same as 'paid employment' – nor is paid employment a definition of the worth of a human being. Often these days someone who does not have paid employment is thought of by others in the same community as being of less worth or significance ('redundant'). To be unemployed, in that secular economic sense of not receiving payment for my work, should mean no more than that I am engaged upon some other important form of work. I am certainly never redundant.

'We headed the procession when it took what we see now to be the wrong turning down into the deep bog of greedy industrialism where money and machines are of more importance than men and women. It is for us to find the way out again, into the sunshine.'
J. B. Priestley, English Journey, 1934

The primary focus of teaching about paid work in much of the church at present emphasises the point that those of us who are seeking to model Christ in our place of paid employment should be considered to be on the cutting edge of evangelism and should be nurtured and encouraged accordingly. That is right and good. However, there is another level which must not be forgotten. Whatever we are working at, no matter how we spend our time, we should do so because we believe that this what God has called us to do. Many of us have lost our understanding of the meaning of 'vocation'. George Mueller said:

> We should work because it is the Lord's will concerning us... whether a believer chooses to become a missionary, a teacher, a carpenter or a businessman, he will be blessed and find satisfaction in his career – as long as he works in joyful obedience to the Lord.[40]

There are five clear consequences of this view of work. Firstly, every form of work can be a vocation: there are no limitations to what God may call us to do. However, not every form of work is necessarily our vocation and the challenge goes out to each of us to consider afresh what we do as our paid employment. There is certainly an excitement and a challenge, often, attached to a high-powered or influential or vital job which may not be replicated in the more mundane tasks of life, such as children's bath time, but this does not make one more important in God's eyes than the other. Certainly the role of father is second only to that of husband for a married man – with paid work coming a (poor) third.

Secondly, if when we work we are doing so in response to a calling from God, there can be (by definition) no hierarchical valuation of jobs as the world would propose. One person's paid employment as chief executive of IBM (if that is where they are called) is no more nor less valuable a task than another person's unpaid parenting (if called to do that). Such a view enables us to examine the issue of comparative incomes. We are called to servanthood; it might come with an income.

Thirdly, God will equip us as necessary by his Spirit to do the work which he has prepared for us to do. We may not be successful in the world's eyes, but that is not the point: we are doing what he has asked us to do. The reality, therefore, is that, as Christians, we may well not be materially successful. The choices we face at work may bring us into conflict with a secular world view or with some of the practices at, or the philosophy of, the company for which we work. Compromise is not an option. Do you behave differently at work from the way you do at home? Do you behave differently from others where you work because of your faith?

Fourthly, as we have seen, the work to which we are called and the way that we earn money to survive may be quite different. God may have called you to preach, as he did Paul, but even Paul was a tent-maker to ensure that he earned enough money along the way not to be a burden on others (Acts 18:3, 1 Thessalonians 2:9). We may need to do one thing to earn money in order to do another thing to which we are called. This requires us to look at how much we need to earn for our calling and so whether or not we need to be in full-time paid employment.

Fifthly, there are no careers in the kingdom of God. This is not to say that the search for excellence and achievement are disparaged for they are positively encouraged in the Bible (as seen, for example, in the building of the tabernacle in Exodus 35). Rather, it is to recognise that careers are a human drive, based on personal ambition, and are not a vocation. Indeed, the word 'career' in the sense we understand it today is a mere 200 years old and means, literally 'a profession affording opportunities of advancement'.[41] Along with that, 'job security' is a secular expression. It is unnecessary and meaningless in a spiritual context (like 'financial security'). One of the differences between a person whose hope is in Jesus and an unbeliever in the workplace is that we know what the future ultimately holds. Our task is to live in the present and to lead others into the promise of that same eternal security.

A final issue to consider is whether wage-employment, even though this has become all-pervasive, is in fact second best to self-employment. To the extent that we have no realistic choice, wage-employment is about us having to sell our labour to enable another person to make a profit. As such we are enslaved and do not have the same opportunities as that person to make our own choices and to be responsible (and, of course, the reverse is true if we are the employer).

'One spiritual discipline we must try to recover is to enjoy tasks instead of simply viewing them as things to get done.'
Dee Dee Risher, Northwest Institute, II–10

As Micah 4:4 puts it, there will come a time, after our swords have been beaten into plowshares, when 'Everyone will sit under their own vine and under their own fig-tree, and no-one will make them afraid, for the Lord Almighty has spoken'.

The structures of the free-market economy and the thrust of globalisation are based largely on the view that wage-employment is the norm and self-employment the exception. Might that not be contested? Again, such a norm is a relatively new concept. Capitalism, or the free market economy, can take many forms. Huge, unaccountable, distantly-run corporations, substantially run by and for the board and the shareholders is a very new form of capitalism. Is it really the only way forward?[42]

There are no simple answers and our work is often not ideal because we are in the world - albeit not 'of' it. Nonetheless, there is an opportunity here for us all to re-assess our current work situations and allow ourselves to consider some fresh alternatives.

Discussion

As you discuss these questions together, do remember that there may be some in your group who may be 'unemployed' or who are in other situations (for example, retired, looking after children or parents at home).

- Look at the story of Joseph (Genesis Chapters 37–47, but don't try to read all of it in your group time!):
  - Why was Joseph called to his work?
  - What example does Joseph provide?
  - Is he the only character in the Bible who is called to create wealth?

- What is the purpose of work?

- Why do you do what you do to earn money?

- Have any of you faced periods of unemployment (in the sense of being without a wage)? How did it make you feel and why?

- As you simplify your time and simplify your money, what implications does that have on the work you are doing?

- Can a company be socially responsible? Should it give money to charity? Should it encourage its employees into good works during work hours? From which corporate pocket should such activity be paid for?

- How does God view work?

Action

- Is there an attitude about work which you need to change? Change it!

- Check with the Lord that you are doing what he wants you to be doing.

'Suffice to say that we all found it extremely stimulating, challenging and useful. I think I can say with confidence that lives have been changed and continue to change. Personally I enjoyed the course and have found a certain sense of release in a number or areas.'

'To the Lord your God belong the heavens, even the highest heavens, the earth and everything in it. Yet the Lord set his affection on your forefathers and loved them, and he chose you, their descendants, above all the nations, as it is today.'
Deuteronomy 10:14–15

Homework

Take some time by yourself to consider these questions:

- Do you feel you have enough time with God, your partner/family/friends?
- Do you have enough time for yourself, to spend on hobbies, gardening and leisure or just to relax?
- Does the time you spend on work allow you to have time to enjoy the money you earn, spend it or invest it prudently? Or is it taking too much out of you?
- Do you believe your pattern of work is giving you health or stress problems?
- How are your general energy levels? Are you chronically or permanently tired? Do you have time to exercise?
- Do you look forward to going to work in the mornings?
- Do you feel your work truly reflects your values?
- Are you happy with the contribution you are making to society?
- Do you think you would be happier if your career changed direction completely?
- Do you feel that, because of your commitments, other people – cleaner, nanny, babysitter, gardener – are impinging too much into your personal life?
- Do you spend much of your time fantasising about your next holiday and then collapse with fatigue when you get there?

As a result of the above thoughts – what changes could you make to your lifestyle?

Further Reading and Resources

- Dominguez and Robin, *Your Money or Your Life* (Penguin, 1999).
- Graham Dow, *A Christian Understanding of Daily Work*, Grove Booklets P57 (Grove Books Ltd.)
- John Goldingay and Robert Innes, God at Work Part I and James Allcock, Robert Innes and David Sheppard, God at Work Part II, Grove Booklets E94 and E96. (Grove Books Ltd.)
- Tom Sine, *Mustard Seed Vs. McWorld, Reinventing Christian Life for a New Millennium*, (Monarch, 1995) for a challenging look at the changing face of the marketplace and how we can respond.
- The Institute for Contemporary Christianity offers many resources for Christians in the workplace: www.licc.org.uk

'Normal is getting dressed in clothes that you buy for work, driving through traffic in a car that you are still paying for, in order to get to the job you need so you can pay for the clothes, car and the house that you leave empty all day in order to afford to live in it.'
Ellen Goodman, quoted in Janet Luhrs, The Simple Living Guide

Notes

Notes

SESSION SEVEN

Caring for God's World

'The Lord God took the man and put him in the Garden of Eden to work it and take care of it' (Genesis 2:15).

Goals

- To begin to consider our responsibility as Christians for the created world.
- To become aware of the statistics which show how swiftly the created order is being degraded.
- To consider how these statistics might change our lifestyle.

Reading

Do you ever take the time to stand outside in the dark on a summer's night and watch the shooting stars, or go to the beach in the rain and feel the power of the sea, or walk around your area noticing the flowers and plants in the gardens around you? There is so much pleasure waiting to be discovered in the smell of the buddleia bush by the road or the sound of the blackbird on the fence. What a beautiful world we live in! Part of living a more simple lifestyle is having the space to notice and enjoy the world that God has created and having the desire to look after it.

In the light of this, read the following statistics. We make no apologies for the lengthy (and somewhat esoteric) list that follows. Give the numbers time to speak for themselves. As we have said before, we do not want you to be overwhelmed, or feel condemned by these figures, but rather to allow these facts to shed light on the situation we find ourselves in, before we go on to look at how we can respond.

Statistics

We are part of the 20% that uses 86% of the world's resources.

If the world's 225 richest people gave 4% of their wealth they could wipe out poverty altogether. (World Development Movement 1999).

Climate change (caused by greenhouse gas emissions, especially carbon dioxide) is the biggest problem facing our world, contributing to many of the 'natural' disasters that have claimed so many lives. Incredibly, more people become refugees through environmental disasters than for any other reason. It is reckoned that there are at least 25 million environmental refugees today. It is estimated that these numbers could double by 2010.[43]

Deforestation is the second highest contributor to climate change, behind that of burning fossil fuels, and is responsible for 20% to 30% of all carbon dioxide in the atmosphere. All the primary (original) rainforests in India, Bangladesh, Sri Lanka and Haiti have been destroyed. Some 2.4 acres of forest is destroyed every second; 149 acres every minute; 214,000 acres each day (larger than New York City) and 78 million acres each year (larger than Poland). The rainforests

'We face a painful choice. To maintain and expand out our material abundance, we are polluting our air and water, and destroying our lands and forests. We simply cannot continue these present economic patterns, and reduce global poverty and preserve a liveable planet all at the same time. We could choose both justice for the poor and a liveable planet – but only if we give up rampant materialism and make hard choices to reverse the environmental destruction.'
Ron Sider, Rich Christians

of the Ivory Coast have almost been completely destroyed. The Philippines lost 55% of its forests between 1960 and 1985 and, by 1985, Thailand had lost 45%. (Rainforest Action Network factsheets.)

It is calculated that 10% of the world's species could disappear within twenty-five years because of the breakdown of rainforest ecosystems. The authoritative 2002 Red List of Threatened Species reports that 11,167 creatures face extinction. This is already 121 more species since the 2000 edition. A third of the world's primate species face a serious risk of extinction. (2002 IUCN Red List of Threatened Species and Conservation International and the Primate Specialist Group of the IUCN.)

Estimated annual cost for clean water and sanitation for everyone on the planet: £5.5 billion. Annual European expenditure on ice cream: £6.6 billion. (United Nations Development Programme: 1998 Human Development Report.)

In the UK, we throw away 165 million tonnes of waste every year and just under 90% of our rubbish is buried in landfill sites. Disposable nappies account for 4% of all UK domestic waste. Eight million of them are thrown away every day and it takes up to 500 years for each one to decompose, while the plastic never disappears.

The Transport Ministry forecast in 2002 that by 2030 there will be 500 million plane passengers a year. The problems are immense; climate change from the carbon dioxide emissions (air travel is the fastest growing source of emissions), health risks from toxic nitrogen oxide emissions, noise pollution and development pressures with road traffic congestion and greenfield sites tarmacced over for runways and car parks. (From R. Valerio, L is for lifestyle: Christian Living that Doesn't Cost the Earth)

There are 480 million cars in the world and nearly 29 million new cars are made each year. Car traffic is expected to increase by 22% by 2010. Of those 480 million, 90% are owned by the sixteen wealthiest countries (one-fifth of the world's population). In the UK we use the car more and more for our shorter journeys. Some 25% of car trips are under two miles and 61% are under five miles. (From Friends of the Earth factsheet)

In contrast to the health problems caused by driving, a regular adult cyclist shows the fitness levels of a person ten years younger. There are an estimated 22 million bikes in the UK with only five million regularly being used. Cycling accounts for only 2% of journeys. If we could raise our figure to 18% we would save 10 million tonnes of carbon dioxide. (From R. Valerio, L is for lifestyle: Christian Living that Doesn't Cost the Earth)

The statistics we have just read demonstrate what an immensely complicated and massive problem we are facing when we look at the environment. There is an urgent need for us all to grasp the nettle and begin to respond, both by campaigning and by making changes in our own lives. It is a sad fact, however, that as Christians we have been very slow in doing so. We have often played down the importance of concern for the environment, and have often looked upon those who demonstrate such a concern as being a bit weird.

There are a number of different reasons as to why this has been the case. Sometimes it is because we are so overwhelmed by the scale of the problem that it leads to paralysis, or because we are too lazy to do anything about it! However, much of our failure to respond adequately has been down to an issue of theology. In particular, there are four beliefs that the church has held which has prevented it from responding and which need re-assessing.[44]

The first is a dualistic world view, a problem that the church has been wrestling with right from its early contact with Greek philosophy. Dualism teaches an unhealthy separation between body and spirit, earth and heaven, natural and spiritual, reason and religion, and so on. It inherently exalts the latter in each of these cases and denigrates the former. The result is that nature or creation is thought to be inferior to the supernatural realm. The important thing, therefore, is to focus one's attention on 'heavenly/spiritual' matters rather than concerning oneself with what goes on 'down here'.

'We tolerate a high rate of waste and then try to cope with the problem of recycling. Would it not be more intelligent first of all to try and reduce the rate of waste? The recycling problem may then itself become much more manageable.'
E. F. Schumacher, This I Believe

The second wrong belief, which flows from an unhealthy dualism, is a hierarchical understanding of Creation. This sees 'God, whose nature is pure spirit, at the top, and the earth, whose nature is material, at the bottom'.[45] The rest of creation, from humanity to animals and plants and so on, are ranged in between in descending importance. As we will see later, there is some truth in this. However, if the earth is seen as distant from God and therefore of little value to him, the consequences are obvious.

The third belief is anthropocentrism – the belief that everything revolves around humanity and was made for our benefit. This has come about through a misunderstanding of the account of Creation and, in particular, of the words 'dominion' and 'subdue' in Genesis 1:28. Again, we shall see that there is some truth in teaching a distinction between humanity and the rest of creation but not when this leads to legitimising domination and oppression rather than stewardship and caring.

The fourth wrong belief is in an otherworldly orientation whereby our real life is not actually here on earth, but begins when we 'get to heaven'. This is captured by the idea of us 'only visiting this planet' and stems from an eschatology that teaches that this world will be completely destroyed at the end of time, and thus there is little point bothering with it now. Again, there is some truth behind such statements of belief but, with this view, God is only interested in 'saving souls' and there is no room for a larger view of salvation which includes the whole of his Creation.

If these four beliefs are wrong, what then is a right understanding of creation and of our role within it?[46] It will not come as a surprise that we start with the assertion that God saw all that he created and declared it 'very good'. In contrast to much of the above, the whole of creation carries within it the intrinsic value of being something that God has made and finds pleasure in. Because he has made it, it belongs to him, first and foremost, and only to humanity secondarily. While we are appointed to govern on his behalf, it is only through his continuing participation that the earth is sustained. One of the key biblical principles arising out of this is that the right of all to use the earth's resources comes before the right of any to ownership.[47] The earth, therefore, has not been given to us as something that God no longer cares about, but as a gift which we are to treasure and look after.

As stewards, there *is* a distinction between humanity and the rest of creation and we have clearly been given a leading role in its governance. However, this should not be taken beyond its limits. Humanity is also very much a part of Creation and thus we cannot take too superior an attitude or exploit it for selfish ends. Hughes says that 'we are fundamentally made of the same material and subject to the same physical conditions. If we damage non-human creation we damage ourselves'.[48]

In Session 2 we saw the result of humanity turning away from God and choosing to go its own way and the results that followed from that.[49] The Fall changed our relationship both with God and also with the rest of Creation which would now carry within it both the curse and blessing of God. However, the rest of the Bible tells the story of his plan for our salvation. Israel is called to be his people and model his purposes for stewardship and there is a particular relationship with the land that acts as a spiritual barometer of her obedience (for example, Deuteronomy 30:15–16; Isaiah 5:8–10; Jeremiah 5:23–25).

God's plan for his Creation finds its fulfilment in Jesus, who affirms creation by choosing to become flesh and by dying and being raised to life again, and who thus brings potential healing to every broken relationship. It is crucial to see that God's intention for salvation involves the whole of creation, not just humanity alone (Romans 8:22, Ephesians 1:9–10; Colossians 1:15–20). Michael Lloyd, in writing about the doctrine of Creation, explains it like this:

> 'It is not just human beings that are valued, though we do have a special value as those creatures who have been made in the image of God. We are worth more than many sparrows, says Jesus (Matthew 10:29, Luke 12:7), but that only provides the reassurance Jesus intends if sparrows themselves are of intrinsic worth. And though they are two-a-penny in the market – and probably the only meat that poor people could afford – Jesus insists that every one of them is the object of God's providential concern. Creation is not declared to be very good until

'The Christian message should offer us a lens through which we can view eternity and see the actions and decisions we take today as ripples on the lake of time which will reach the shores of future generations for good or ill.'
Michael Bates

human beings are a part of it (Genesis 1:31), but every stage and every part of Creation is assessed as being good in the eyes of its Maker. Creation has an intrinsic value of its own.

Our planet has paid a high price for the way in which we have forgotten this truth, and failed to treat Creation as valuable. In practice [we have acted on the basis that] Creation has no intrinsic purpose and we may therefore impose our own purposes on it; and that Creation has no intrinsic worth beyond what it is worth to us. In the Eighties, the British Secretary of State for the Environment (of all people!) proposed the privatisation of nature reserves – as if the only value they possess is their financial potential. [In fact], they have value in their own right because there is a person behind the universe who made it and values it.' [50]

Revelation 4 gives us a glimpse of the future to which all of God's Creation is orientated: the future that is begun with the 'first fruits' of the resurrection. 'The new creation is not a replacement for the present world but is the eschatological future of this world'.[51] So the role to which we are called is a great privilege, but also an awesome responsibility. As Gunton says, 'we human creatures are the centre of the world's problems, and only by our redirection will the whole Creation be set free'.[52]

The Bible ends with a wonderful picture of the new heaven and the new earth, both of which have significant continuity with the heaven and earth that exist now (Revelation 21–22).[53] So, the new Jerusalem comes down from heaven – we do not 'go up there' – and creation is restored, not replaced. All things are made new in Jesus: this involves all of Creation and the final end to the curse. Too often our view of the end times ('eschatology') has been used as an excuse for inaction regarding looking after God's world. This couldn't be further from the truth! As we see how God's plans involve all of creation, so we must long to play our part in bringing this about. It is our future hope that inspires us to work for its present realisation.

Finally, we must note again the link between humanity and the environment. It is wrong in our present situation to try to play off a concern for the environment against a concern for people - as many have tried to do. What is abundantly clear in our global situation is that the two are intricately linked, and that when creation is being abused, it is invariably the poor who suffer as a result. If we are concerned about issues of justice and oppression then we must be prepared to wrestle with the issues of our God-given environment.

Discussion

- Read Colossians 1:1–23.
  - Jesus' death was not only for the sake of people, but was also for 'all things on earth and in heaven' (v.20). Is that a new concept for you? How does it help you understand your responsibility for God's world?
  - How can we 'proclaim the gospel to every creature under heaven' (v.23)?
- Go through the 'What on Earth am I Doing?' questionnaire in Appendix 4. Discuss together what issues it raises. Please note the spirit in which it was written: it is meant to be light-hearted, like a quiz in a magazine! Not every question will be applicable to every person and it is not meant as a legalistic list of things to do.
- How aware are you of the beauty of the things that are around you? For example, do you ever stop to smell a flower or watch a bird fly? If, as a result of earlier sessions, you are beginning to walk or cycle more instead of driving, then you may naturally have found this happening more often.
- Look at the quote from Ron Sider at the foot of the first page of this Session. What is your response to what he says?
- As a Christian do you feel comfortable with your approach to the environment?
- If you are aware that you are not as concerned about environmental issues as you should be, why do you think that is?
- What steps should you take?
- Do you ever get involved in environmental campaigns? What do you do? If not, why not?

'The heavens declare the glory of God;
The skies proclaim the work of his hands'
Psalm 19:1–2

Action

Begin to put into action some of the things you have discussed. Consider which of the issues particularly affects you or to which you have a particular response. Work out how you could set about finding out more about it/them and set yourself a timetable to do so.

Homework

Take an issue that is of particular concern to you (perhaps taken from the statistics above or from the lifestyle Audit) and find out how you can get involved with it (for example, by writing to your MP or your local council). Friends of the Earth are very helpful with ideas (www.foe.co.uk).

OR: Write a letter to your great-great-great-grandchild. Visualise the child opening it somewhere in the twenty second century. This is a real life assignment and you can actually arrange for the letter to be delivered. You could write things like this:

1. Describe to your descendant what the world is like for you now.
2. Describe what worries you about the future and what you do to assure the future for your descendants.
3. What are your concerns for the world that your descendants would inherit?
4. What do you imagine the world of 2100 AD to be like?
5. Based on your experience of life in the twentieth century, what would you pass along to your descendant by way of 'sage advice'?

Now in your imagination, return to this time and the place you are in. What has writing this letter meant to you? What are you feeling and thinking about?[54]

OR: Visit your local landfill. Find out how long before it will reach capacity and what will be done when it is full. Count the number of bin bags you put out each month and try to halve that number!

Further Reading and Resources

- R.J. Berry (ed.), *The Care of Creation* (IVP, 2000).
- R. Valerio, *L is for Lifestyle: Christian Living that Doesn't Cost the Earth.*
- A Rocha: www.arocha.org
- Christian Ecology Link: www.Christian-ecology.org.uk
- Friends of the Earth website, publications and membership magazine (www.foe.org.uk)
- Going for Green: Gfg@dircon.co.uk www.gfg.iclnet.co.uk
- James Jones, *Jesus and the Earth* (SPCK, 2003).

'St Francis was a man who did not want to see the wood for the trees. He wanted to see each tree as a separate and almost sacred thing.'
G. K. Chesterton

Notes

Notes

SESSION EIGHT

More Money Matters

Come, all you who are thirsty,
come to the waters;
and you who have no money,
come, buy and eat!
Come, buy wine and milk
without money and without cost.
Why spend money on what is not bread,
and your labour on what does not satisfy?
Listen, listen to me, and eat what is good,
And your soul will delight in the richest of fare.
Give ear and come to me;
Hear me, that your soul may live. (Isaiah 55:1–3)

Goals

- To think through our choices concerning difficult money issues.
- To enlarge our understanding of giving.

Reading

In Sessions 3 and 4 we laid a biblical foundation for our understanding of money and possessions and then began to explore some of the principles for our use of it today. In this session we are going to look further into some of the very practical decisions that we have to make in our lives about what we do with our money: saving, credit and debt, giving, investment and mortgages.

The issues that we look at may be quite personal to us and it may come as a surprise that we should even consider these things from a new perspective. What will become clear is that, as Christians, we have a lot of hard thinking to do on these topics. Too often we have just followed our society's economic patterns and structures without asking ourselves if there might be other models we could adopt or initiate which would more adequately reflect the values of the kingdom of God. Because these topics are so big, we can only begin to scratch the surface in this session. Many of the questions raised do not have simple answers and there are suggestions for follow-up reading. Some of us will leave this session with immediate challenges and things we know we have to do. For others, our thinking here will begin a process which we will be working on for many years. Whatever the outcome, we would encourage you to be as open and undefensive in your discussion as possible. Let us remember too that here, perhaps more than ever, we must seek to ensure that we are operating within an atmosphere of grace.

'The first Christians did not share their goods in a free and full manner till after the bomb of the Spirit exploded in their souls... To say, "this is yours, not mine" and to carry the words into effect, is as much a miracle of God as raising of the dead.'
James K. Baxter, quoted in David Watson **Discipleship**

Before we turn to the specific topics, however, let us pause a moment to consider the economic world in which we are operating: a capitalist free-market economy. In many ways this has proven to be the best system that has been found: it has certainly generated wealth for many people in many countries. However, in the form in which it is being practised today, it can be seen to be encouraging the breakdown of the family and of community and thus it will lead ultimately to social disintegration. It also increases the gap between poor and rich because it does not allow the poor access to the resources they need to earn a living, nor does it allow them to compete on equal terms with the rich.[54] The unhealthy bias in modern day capitalism can be summed up in the words of E.F. Schumacher: 'out of the large number of aspects which in real life have to be seen and judged together before a decision can be taken, economics supplies one – whether a thing yields a money profit to those who undertake it or not'.

In response to this, the concept of Corporate Social Responsibility (CSR) has emerged in the business community. David Batstone, in Saving the Corporate Soul, suggests eight principles of CSR:

1. The directors and executives of a company will align their personal interests with those of stakeholders and act in a responsible way to ensure the viability of the enterprise.

2. A company's business operations will be transparent to shareholders, employees, and the public, and its executives will stand by the integrity of their decisions.

3. A company will think of itself as part of a community as well as a market.

4. A company will represent its products honestly to customers and honour their dignity up to and beyond transaction.

5. The worker will be treated as a valuable team member, not just a hired hand.

6. The environment will be treated as a silent stakeholder, a party to which the company is wholly accountable.

7. A company will strive for balance, diversity, and equality in its relationships with workers, customers, and suppliers.

8. A company will pursue international trade and production based on respect for the rights of workers and citizens of trade partner nations.[56]

CSR provides the Christian with the opportunity to work within existing structures. However it is sometimes necessary to consider building new structures. Mother Mary Claire of the Sisters of the Love of God says, 'we live in a time when things are unravelling. If you know anything about weaving, you know that things which are unravelling cannot be patched. Our task in this period of unravelling is not to patch the old patterns but to build the loom on which the new patterns are woven'. We each and together need to attempt that loom-building because the world will continue on its path towards increasing inequality and social breakdown unless an alternative model can be shown to be successful.

There is always a danger in proposing a new economic model and we must remember that nothing in this present age will be perfect. However, there is a desperate need for a vision which offers hope for the ever-increasing numbers of the poor and excluded. The tenets of the vision of FACE to Face (mentioned in the foreword) are:

1. Self-employment is the norm and wage-employment the necessary exception.

2. Businesses take into account the needs of the wider community.

3. Businesses are owned locally and are locally accountable.

4. Broadly equal value is given to all work.

'For riches and abundance come hypocritically clad in sheep's clothing pretending to be security against anxieties and they become then the object of anxiety... they secure a man against anxieties just about as well as the wolf which is put to tending the sheep secures them against the wolf'
Richard Forster, Celebration of Discipline

5. Trustworthiness and fairness are at the heart of all business dealings.

6. Business activity is consistent with our role as stewards of God's creation.

With these six principles in mind, let us now turn to consider some of those specific financial issues that we have to face during the course of our lives.

1. Saving and Insurance [57]

Should a Christian save and, if so, what is an appropriate level? Does saving anything demonstrate a lack of faith in God's provision or does not saving demonstrate a lack of prudence and good stewardship? The Bible seems to teach both and often the good example given of the ant that 'stores its provisions in summer and gathers its food at harvest' (Proverbs 6:8) is contrasted with Jesus' command that you should not 'store up for yourselves treasures on earth' (Matthew 6:19).

There would seem, biblically, to be two positive grounds given for savings and insurance: firstly, in order to fulfil one's family obligations (Mark 7:9–13; 1 Tim. 5:8) and, secondly, in order not to be dependent on anyone (2 Thessalonians 3:6–12). Alongside this is the continual and overarching reminder that we must be open-handed with any money or possessions we have to help the poor (eg Ephesians 4:28). This, of course, still leaves room for hugely varying interpretations as to what that means. How far does our family extend? How much should we leave our children? What about provision for elderly parents? How much do I need to live on in order to avoid dependence? In this, as with so much, the Bible's teaching gives us parameters but then does not provide us with a single universally applicable norm. It is likely that this, actually, is divinely intended and the New Testament would seem to teach that the appropriate attitude to wealth depends to some extent on the Christian's situation and calling (for example, to the mission field, to a dependent family or to singleness).

We must remember at all times that it is our natural inclination to hold on to as much as we can 'just in case'! A rainy day does not necessarily mean a storm-ridden decade. As we saw in our earlier sessions, the Bible is full of warnings about the dangers of wealth and its accumulation. We must always guard ourselves against the desire to accumulate as much as possible in order to make ourselves as secure as possible: 'rejection of the worship of Money must result in a lower level of financial accumulation than would otherwise be the case… . The need to avoid pure hoarding, and bondage to possessions, implies that Christians need to be crystal clear about the purpose for which they are saving, or continuing to own valuable assets (eg a large house). Once that purpose has been achieved, saving should cease and the surplus given away'.[58] In the story of the rich young ruler which we looked at in Session 4, the man missed the key to what Jesus was offering: the opportunity to live in a community where there was more than enough for everyone and where he could learn to love and love deeply by being loved and loved deeply. In a community such as that described in Acts 2 and 4, the need to save and to insure substantially falls away.

2. Credit and Debt

If you make a £1,000 purchase on a credit card charging 18% interest and make only minimum payments each month, that purchase will cost approximately £1,400. That's 40% more than the purchase price! If credit cards tempt you, destroy all but one. Or consider freezing (yes, freezing) your credit cards in containers of ice so that, to use them, you have to wait for the ice to thaw.
(Centre for A New American Dream)

The idea of credit is, of course, a misnomer like 'life' insurance. What we are really talking about here is debt. Using credit unwisely has become one of the biggest financial problems of our society. Nearly every day the post brings more tempting offers of credit cards and their facilities, offering 'good' rates of interest and various rewards such as air miles; those cards we do use regularly raise our credit limits, thus encouraging us to spend more and get ever more into debt.

'I've learned that we must hold everything loosely, because when I grip it tightly,
it hurts when the Father prises my fingers loose and takes it from me.'
Corrie ten Boom

While borrowing is permitted in the Bible it does still contain warnings against going into debt (eg Proverbs 22:7; 17:18). As Burkitt says, 'regardless of how it seems today, debt is not normal in any economy and should not be normal for God's people'.[59] Unless we have a cast iron will, we should be extremely careful about using credit cards (and that also applies to store cards). The same is true of bank overdrafts. In reality, we are spending money that we do not have and, while our society encourages this and tells us it is fine, we should resist the pressure at all times. Debit cards (like Switch), are much the preferable option as the money goes out of our account almost immediately.

If we do find ourselves in a situation where our finances have got out of our control, then we must take action. A good idea is to contact Credit Action (www.creditaction.com) or Christians Against Poverty (www.CAPuk.org) – both Christian organisations that help people in such situations, as well as providing excellent advice on a whole variety of financial topics.[60]

Some suggestions:

- Ask yourself, do I really need a credit card (or so many)?
- Pay off all your credit card debts as soon as you can.
- Cancel all but one credit card for emergency use. Keep the card with the lowest annual fee.
- If you need to buy something large, save up for it rather than buy it on credit. You can then use the money you are saving positively by, for example, investing it in an ethical bank / microcredit organisation or lending it to someone who needs it and can repay you (at no interest) in the time in which you need it.
- If you have to keep a credit card, ensure it is one which benefits a charity when you use it.
- If you still want to use a credit card, only do so on the understanding that you pay off your entire credit each month, rather than paying it off in instalments and paying interest.
- Get rid of all your store cards.
- Discipline your finances so you do not use your overdraft.
- Before you buy anything on credit ask yourself these questions: Do I really need this item? Do I need it now? What benefit will it bring me/my family? Has advertising/peer pressure played a part in this decision? Can I delay buying this until I can afford to pay cash for it? Will this purchase increase my levels of credit to dangerous levels?[61]
- Consider within the group whether or not some members might be able to pay off the debts of others or otherwise reduce a debt burden on a brother or a sister in Christ.

3. Giving

Matthew 6:1–4 tells us that giving is one of the main spiritual disciplines, essential for the maintenance of a healthy spiritual life. Never does the Bible teach that it is an optional extra for those with enough surplus money. As we saw from our look at the Old Testament in Session Three, our attitude towards giving is built on two pillars. Firstly, what God has done for us, both through the Exodus of the children of God, and then through the supreme Exodus – that which Jesus' death and resurrection brought, the ultimate gift (John 3:16); and secondly, the understanding that everything we have belongs to God and so should be available to others.

Discussions on giving generally revolve around whether or not it is biblical to tithe, by which is usually meant to give 10 per cent of your income (whether net or gross). The tithing system in the Old Testament is in reality not so clear or easy to pin down to such a neat figure. Scholars think that actually the tithing system, all in all, amounted to a good 25 per cent of the people's income. Either way, while tithing can be a helpful guideline, there is no clear New Testament mandate for tithing. Rather what comes through is an attitude of far more generous extravagance in one's giving (2 Corinthians 9:6–7). The emphasis is not so much on how much we should give, but on how much it is right for us to keep.

'If our goods are not available to the community they are stolen goods.'
Martin Luther

According to Stuart Murray,

> 'tithing is simply not radical enough for the kingdom of God. Costly decsions are needed that will involve living more simply, moving into smaller houses and into run-down neighbourhoods, redistributing resources across the world church, investing capital as well as income in kingdom projects, being and preaching good news to the poor. Becoming rich honestly is no barrier to following Jesus, but retaining wealth in a world of poverty, hunger and suffering surely is. Discipleship that is truly Jesus-centred cannot be content with tithing. Restoration of New Testament Christianity will involve a much more radical approach'. [62]

There are two particular places in which we receive some guidance on giving. The first is in 1 Corinthians 16:1–2. Here we are told that our giving should be a priority: it should be regular; everyone should give and it should be proportionate. The second place is in 2 Corinthians 8–9. This gives a wonderful picture of what a giving church should look like. Read this description of the early church, given by Aristides in 125 AD. He was not a Christian. He says:

> They walk in all humility and kindness, and falsehood is not found among them, and they love one another. They don't despise the widow and don't upset the orphan. He who has gives liberally to he who has not. If they see a stranger, they bring him under their roof and rejoice over him, as if it were their own brother: for they call themselves brethren, not after the flesh, but after the spirit and in God; but when one of their poor passes away from the world, and any of them see him, then he provides for his burial according to his ability; and if they hear that any of their number is imprisoned or oppressed for the name of their Messiah, all of them provide for his needs, and if it is possible that he may be delivered, they deliver him. And if there is among them a person who is poor and needy, and they have not an abundance of necessaries, they fast two or three days that they may supply the needy with their necessary food.

If we are sorting out our budget, using credit wisely (or not at all) and rethinking our savings, then we have a wonderful opportunity to give more of our money away. Only when we discover the excitement, the sheer – almost selfish – pleasure, that there is in giving, shall we know the extraordinary freedom that Christ promises.

4. Investment

In many churches, financial issues are hardly ever talked about and, if they are, then it will almost invariably be about giving to the church. It is too easy to be under the impression that all God is concerned about is that we give away some of our money and then the rest of it is ours to do with as we will. This session (and Session 4) should lead us towards a recognition that God is concerned not just about the money we give but also about what we do with the money we keep.

Nowhere is this insight more salient than in the question of investment. If we were to ask anybody why they invested, whether Christian or not, the reply would no doubt be that we invest in order to make more money to become more financially secure. The fact that there would be little difference between a Christian's and a non-Christian's answer (except perhaps in a vague understanding of stewardship) should alert us to the possibility that we need to do some serious thinking around this issue.

It would be quite easy to think that the Bible does not teach us much about how or where to invest. However, it is here that we bring in some of the insights that we have gained so far and it will readily be seen that Scripture does in fact provide us with a number of principles that can helpfully guide us. There are three main areas for consideration here. Firstly, the backdrop to this section must be to form a view on how God sees private property. The key here is that I do not own anything, and whatever I hold as a steward is God's to do with as he chooses. Once my needs are satisfied, everything else is likely to be needed by others. So private property over and above my needs is subordinate to the needs of the community. So, for instance, it is legitimate to save in order to avoid dependence on others and to be able to make appropriate provision for one's family. Such savings will almost inevitably take the form of investments of one sort or another (including pensions, mortgages over property – the value of which is increasing over time – and insurance).

'Our economic, political and social systems are responsible for much of the world's human suffering and ecological destruction. These systems must be totally transformed to ways of living that are decentralised, ecological, just, and joyful.'
Susan Meeker-Lowry, Invested in the Common Good

Secondly, we have looked at the six pillars that might go to make up a new economic vision, including local ownership and accountability, and nothing that conflicts with our role as stewards of God's creation. A further aspect of the FACE to Face vision, and one with clear biblical endorsment, is that loans to the poor for the start-up and expansion of their businesses should be interest-free. [63]

A third, new, principle can be added here: that of not reaping where one has not sown (taken from Luke 19:21). By this is meant that there should be a proper sharing of reward between those involved in a business activity to ensure that risks are appropriately rewarded and that no-one takes the fruit of someone else's labour. One of the core reasons for the increasing divisions between poor and rich, both in industrialised and in developing nations, is that capital and land owners are reaping a reward all or part of which may not be theirs to reap as they are not taking a risk commensurate with this return. [64]

If these principles are followed, it will be apparent how starkly they stand in contrast to the accepted forms of investment that most of us as Christians follow today. So, for example, shareholdings are too often in large companies where there is no local accountability or relational basis and dividends are often used as the means of making profit. Banks, likewise, give the depositor no control over the use of their finances nor over how the bank conducts its relationships with its borrowers. [65] Yet we are rewarded by payments of interest from these activities. Will we be prepared to ask ourselves the hard questions about our investments and begin to consider alternative ways to use our money?[66]

A further note needs to be made about ethical investments. The capitalist culture in which we are living is only interested in profit. As Mills says, 'consult any financial adviser about where to put your savings and four things will guide their counsel – risk, return, personal circumstance and tax. It is unlikely that the ethical status of your investments will enter into their calculations'.[67] And yet, as Christians, we have a responsibility to ensure that any money we have is not being used to the detriment either of other people or of the environment. It is up to us to take the initiative to find out about the companies that we are investing in, remembering that ethical does not just mean negatively not investing in things such as the arms trade, but also means investing into businesses which are contributing positively to issues of fair trade, human rights, the environment and local community development [68] and which are not so large, or governed from such a distance, that they are not locally accountable. As we do this, how exciting it is to think of the potential for our money to benefit so many people!

5. Mortgages

Most of us in the UK wanting to buy a property will need to have a mortgage and, for many, that option is actually cheaper than renting. The problem with this is that the cost of our housing eats up so much of our monthly budget that it leaves little left for other things.

The ideal (and biblically preferred) position is for us to be debt-free and hence not to have a mortgage, but the reality in the UK today is very different. The best stewardship position then is to aim to become debt-free and pay off the mortgage as soon as possible so that we might have more control over the money we have been given for which we act as steward. How might this happen? Firstly, it could happen more swiftly if we put some of our extra money, or savings, into paying off our mortgage more quickly (this almost invariably being the best form of saving). Secondly, it could happen if we were prepared to live in smaller houses which cost less. Our tendency is to look at how much of a mortgage we are able to get and then buy as big as we can within that price band! Burkett believes that the percentage of an average family's net income that is spent on a house should be no more than 25%. Add to this the cost of utilities, insurance, maintenance and incidentals and it should still not be more than 36%. The problem is that too many people spend upwards of 60% on their house. [69]

If, instead, we were prepared not to follow society's upwardly mobile trend in this regard and buy a smaller house, then we could possibly put down a larger deposit and pay off the mortgage more quickly. Some of what is in these paragraphs will not apply to all of us, particularly if we are key workers or struggling to reach the bottom rung of the property ladder in London or the South-East. However, there will be some of us reading this who, if we are honest, can say that

> *'Most things in life – automobiles, mistresses, cancer – are important principally to those who have them. Money, in contrast, is equally important to those who have it and those who don't. Both, accordingly, have a concern for understanding it. Both should proceed in the full confidence that they can.'*
> *J. K. Galbraith, Money*

we are living in a house that is bigger than we need, paying out large mortgage and utility bills each month. If we were willing to move into smaller accommodation we would release considerable sums of money each month that could be given away or otherwise used more actively for kingdom purposes.

Alongside this is the question of the area in which we live. Again, too many of us follow our society's upwardly mobile trend of moving into bigger homes and out of the less reputable areas, into 'nicer' places with higher house prices. Will the kingdom of God advance further if more Christians are willing to stay or move into the more run-down places to be salt and light there? The Message's EDEN projects, started in 1997, have teams of up to thirty people moving long-term into some of the most deprived estates in Manchester. They are seeing many young people come to faith and families changing as a result of living out the gospel in those places.

A third way of reducing our mortgages is by sharing our homes. This will be looked at more closely in the next session but there are a number of examples of older couples with larger houses with a third storey or a granny annexe. They have been able to allow a single person or two or a younger couple to live with them (fairly independently or not as is the desire) at a reduced or zero rate of rent, thus again freeing up that younger couple's income for saving up for a deposit or giving into the kingdom of God or for enabling them to be more involved with local ministries that cannot pay them a salary.

A fourth way would be for those Christians in a church who have some savings to pool them to purchase property which could be lived in interest-free by singles or couples who cannot afford to buy or rent in that area. The investment would substantially retain its value over the long term and might even increase during such period of occupancy and investors would have the security of property ownership which has historically been sound over the medium term.

Discussion

- As open as we try to be, we often find ourselves becoming defensive when we look at these issues. Why is that?
- Go through each of the sections above, discussing the questions, thoughts and challenges they have raised.

Homework

- Take some time to investigate your investments to find out which companies your money is helping. Don't forget to include your pension in this if you have one.
- Similarly, investigate any investments that your church or denomination might have. Are there areas in which your church or denomination could invest more ethically? The World Development Movement and Christian Aid would be helpful for both of these homework points: www.wdm.org.uk; www.christian-aid.org.uk.

Further Reading and Resources

- Larry Burkett, *Debt-Free Living* (Moody Press, 1999).
- Paul Mills, Faith Versus Prudence? (Cambridge Papers 4:1, The Jubilee Centre, 1995).
- Paul Mills, Investing as a Christian (Cambridge Papers ,The Jubilee Centre,7:1, 1996).

'I beg you, O Jesus most poor, that it may be the distinction of me and mine forevermore, for your name's sake to posses nothing under heaven as our own.'
Words of St Francis – anthology by James Meyer

Notes

Notes

SESSION NINE

Community

'All the believers were one in heart and mind. No-one claimed that any of their possessions were their own but they shared everything they had'. (Acts 4:32)

Goals

- To reach a clearer understanding of what community is.
- To consider some examples of community.
- To be challenged to build community in our churches and in the neighbourhoods around us.

Reading

It has been said that the less we have of community the more we talk about it. Certainly, 'community' has become one of the buzz-words of recent years. Everyone wants it, but no-one really seems to know what it is. What we do know is that we are experiencing less and less of it in our society as the years go by. We are developing an increasingly consumer-driven culture with its emphasis on the individual. And as we become more mobile as a society, so we are losing the traditional structures we once had around us of family and local community/neighbourhood. Many people struggle with feelings of isolation and loneliness and try to find their security in many different ways, ranging from possessions and work to image and sex.

There is a clear role for the church to provide the community that people are longing for and to help one another stand against the negative trends in our society. The Evangelical Commitment to Simple Lifestyle says: 'It is when the new community is most obviously distinct from the world – in its values, standards and lifestyle – that it presents the world with a radically attractive alternative and so exercises its greatest influence for Christ.' [70] It will have become very obvious by now that a simpler lifestyle is by no means simple! To go against the flow of the world around us takes a lot out of us. It will often make our lives more complicated as we have to struggle with the implications of the choices we make. To do this by ourselves is hard. It is not what God intends. Christine Sine says that 'with the mounting pressures of a McWorld future we are all going to need to be in communities of believers amongst whom we are known, loved and held accountable. Building a strong, mutually supportive Christian community committed to mission will be one of the most important tasks for the church in the twenty first century'. [71]

There are good examples of communities in the Bible. The community of prophets in the Old Testament provides us with one such model. In 2 Kings 6:1–3 Elisha and his followers are prepared to listen to God and respond in any way appropriate. Jesus established the apostolic model whereby he spent his three years of ministry sharing himself with his twelve disciples and some women followers. They were united in their commitment to follow Jesus the Messiah and see in the kingdom of God. In addition, the early church in Jerusalem provides a further example of a challenging picture of how they worked together, meeting daily and sharing everything according to need.

'I dream of vibrant neighbourhoods where people relate to each other as neighbours.'
Dave Andrews, Can You Hear the Heartbeat

There are many other examples of Christian communities throughout church history. One of the most notable is the Desert Fathers which began in the monasteries of the Egyptian and Syrian deserts. It was a reaction against the apathy that had become a part of the church. They sought to remove themselves physically from the depravity and temptations of the world, and instead move nearer to God, by living in remote desert areas. [72]

These Desert Fathers directly influenced the Celts who were to bear such a witness to the possibility of living radical community lives. Esther de Waal tells us that 'the prominence given to the Trinity conveys to us something of how these men and women felt about themselves and their world. A God who is Trinity in unity challenges self-centred isolation and points instead to fellowship'.[73] In the face of the Roman church with its hierarchy and worldly power, the Celts sought to develop churches which expressed the perfect community found in the relationship between Father, Son and Holy Spirit. One of the ways in which they sought to do this was by encouraging each member to have an anamchara – a soul friend. This was a more mature person who would guide that member on their spiritual journey through a relationship of openness and accountability.

Many of the Celtic communities continue to this day in places such as Iona and Lindisfarne. Ray Simpson, for example, is the founder of the Community of Aidan and Hilda. This community is 'a body of Christians who wish to live wholeheartedly as disciples of Jesus Christ, and to express this in a distinctive way that draws inspiration from the lives of St. Aidan and other Celtic saints'. They follow the three vows of simplicity, chastity (not celibacy necessarily) and obedience. Each member has a soul friend and they meet twice a year. This friend helps the community member follow a way of life in ten different areas: study and application of the Celtic Christian way; the spiritual journey, including retreats and pilgrimages; a daily rhythm of prayer, work and rest; intercessory prayer; simplicity of lifestyle; care for and affirmation of creation; wholeness not fragmentation; openness to the wind of the Spirit; unity; and, finally, mission (including working with the poor). [74]

Many communities have been started in recent history such as the Celtic example based on the Trinity and fellowship. Many communities were started to serve a particular purpose, such as the L'Abri fellowships – centres for study that were founded by the Shaeffers. There is also Betel International which establishes communities that serve people trying to recover from substance abuse. The L'Arche communities were founded by Jean Vanier to enable people with learning difficulties to live (with assistance) in a loving family environment. There was also Emmaus, which was started in 1949 by Abbe Pierre to provide homeless people with a place to live and work. There are now over 340 Emmaus communities world wide, whose aim is to restore the self-respect and motivation essential to rehabilitating homeless people.

Other communities exist with less specific aims, such as The Community of The Risen Christ in Glasgow. This community describes itself as 'a group of ordinary people from all walks of life, both young and old, seeking to live out our Christian faith in a community context' (www.risenchrist.org.uk). Community needs to start where we are, with the people in our churches. Look back to Aristides' description of the early church in Session Eight (under 'Giving'). This is a wonderful picture of a church living in community together and such a description can become that of our church too.

Jesus said that 'Everyone will know that you are my disciples, if you love one another' (John 13:35). We do not all need to live together in the same building, but we do all need to live with much greater openness and accountability, servanthood and generosity.

We can all start building community in our church and neighbourhood today. For some of us this will mean looking for chances to give time and help. As we do so, we will become more aware of the needs around us by becoming more aware of the people around us! For others it will mean opening our homes and inviting in those who are not usually invited to do anything. It may mean opening our homes to have others live with us, maybe from the church or from the community around us, through fostering schemes and the like (although this is obviously subject to an appropriateness test).

Community also refers to the society of which we are a part and one of our callings as Christians is to be salt and light into that world (Matthew 5:13–16). As we begin to model community between one another so we must not forget our calling to be citizens in the wider world. We all have a responsibility to engage with the structures of that world, whether

> *'In [my] vision of the future, I see connection – vital links of shared experience, understanding and mutual support – between people from all backgrounds. People reaching out across every divide and over every doorstep to share their stories and their talents, confide that everyone has something to give, and unashamed to admit that each of us needs support at some point in our lives.'*
> *Jane Tewson, co-founder of Comic Relief, What If...?*

through campaigning letters or getting involved in the local council or residents' associations. Our call is to model to those around us what it means to be a part of the kingdom of God.

Our supreme model is Jesus, who refused to let boundaries stand in the way of God's love (see, for example, Matt. 8:5–13; John 4 and Luke 8:43–48). Writing on 'loving the stranger', Revd. Dr. Inderjit Bhogal says, 'Jesus has left an example for his community. Practise hospitality. Eat with each other. Eat with the most vulnerable ones. Eat with "the stranger". Our lifestyle should be one of hospitality and solidarity, not hostility and segregation.'[75] As Abraham showed hospitality to the three strangers in Genesis 18, so we too should be ready to open our doors to those who are not like ourselves. Chief Rabbi Jonathan Sacks quotes the Jewish sages who said, 'on only one occasion does the Hebrew Bible command us to love our neighbour, but in 37 places [it] commands us to love the stranger', and he adds: 'The stranger is one we are taught to love precisely because he is not like ourselves.'[76] This is hard because we often fear getting to know people who are different.

The key word here is hospitality. When we use the term 'hospitality' we evoke ideas of warm kindness, tea parties, superficial conversations and 'nice' environments. Hospitality in its truest sense allows us to welcome both friend and stranger into our lives, enabling our journeys to cross and interact with one another. This brings a richness into the lives of both host and guest, where perhaps the separation of even these terms can fade. We find, in that togetherness, a new sense of hospitality emerging.

As we live in community together, hospitality should be at the heart of our lives, both for one another and those beyond. If we can discover this solid and sure hospitality we may touch something of the sense of community that at times eludes us. We might find a place where our histories and experiences enrich one another. This is a place where we can face the struggles of life together; a place where we can get alongside those who are ill and dying and do nothing more than simply be; a place where we can reach beyond to those in need with the love of Christ. It's out of relationship with God that we find space and desire to serve others.

One particularly inspirational model of community today is that of the co-housing movement which began originally in Denmark in the 1970s but has now spread throughout the world, particular in the USA. Co-housing is a type of collaborative housing that attempts to overcome the alienation of modern subdivisions where no-one knows their neighbours and where there is no sense of community. It is characterised by private dwellings with their own kitchen, living-dining room and so on. But there are also extensive common facilities. The common building might include a large dining room, kitchen, lounges, meeting rooms, recreation and childcare facilities, library and workshops. Usually, co-housing communities are designed and managed by the residents, and are intentional neighbourhoods. The people are consciously committed to living as a community. The physical design encourages this and makes social contact both easy and inevitable. The typical co-housing community has twenty to thirty separate family homes along a pedestrian street or clustered around a courtyard. Residents of these communities often have several optional group meals in the common building each week. By virtue of their design and nature, they are environmentally friendly because they reduce energy consumption per household. They are pedestrian-only areas with parking facilities around the edges.[77] While we do not always have the land readily available to us in the UK, unlike the USA, it would still be interesting to consider how we might incorporate some of these co-housing ideas into our communities today.

As will be apparent by now, there is no blue-print for what a community should physically look like, and each of us in our own communities has to struggle to determine how best to determine our values. As inspirational as the various models are in the Bible, through church history and today, we can never seek merely to duplicate them. Christians of each generation have to find their own way of living out community in the light of the implications of being salt and light in their particular world. Nonetheless, Jean Vanier, the founder of L'Arche Communities, does see all true communities as carrying certain hallmarks: 'willingness to be vulnerable; to know one's limitations, weaknesses; to know and be known; to discover our deepest wounds; belonging; listening; being; contemplative prayer. A community has hospitality at its heart; a sect has exclusion at its heart. A leader of community sets members free to follow their own authentic Christ-centred journey; the leader of a sect ties members ever more rigidly to the ways of its founder. A sect has control at its heart; a community has journey at its heart'. [78]

'To do justice to the biblical understanding of the church we must go one step further and say that the goal of evangelism is the formation of Christian community.'
Peter Wagner, The community of the King

Discussion

- Find different examples of community in the Bible and in the history of the church and discuss what lessons can be learned from them (eg the laws of the Old Testament, particularly the Jubilee; Jesus and his disciples; the early church of Acts 2 and 4; the lives of people such as St Francis or Mother Teresa or Jackie Pullinger-To).
- Describe a time when you have been in community (eg family, college halls, church week-end away). What was the core of that experience and what made it feel like community?
- Have a look at Jean Vanier's hallmarks of community in the final paragraph of the reading. How might we work on each of those points in our church today?
- What would be the benefits of having a 'soul-friend'?
- What model of community is your church giving to the wider community?
- Consider the community in which you live. How often do you participate in its activities? If so, what forms does it take?
- What is blocking you from experiencing community today?
- What can you do/are you doing to increase community in your life on a personal and societal level?

Action

Do one thing this week that will contribute to building community, whether in your church or more widely.

Homework

Take time to look further at the different models of community that are around. A good place to start would be by reading some of the Celtic literature to learn more about their way of life and also to look at the websites for the co-housing network and the 'intentional community' network. Look at how you can develop their principles in your own community.

Prayer

Further Reading and Resources

- Tom Sine, *Mustard Seed Vs McWorld* (Monarch, 1995).
- Ray Simpson, *Exploring Celtic Spirituality* (Hodder & Stoughton, 1995).
- Henri Nouwen, *Reaching Out* (Doubleday, 1995).
- Christine Pohl, *Making Room* (Wm B Eerdmans Publishing Co, 1999).
- Co-housing Network: www.cohousing.org
- Intentional Communities: www.ic.org

'They (the twelve disciples) were to share everything together, their joys, their sorrows, their pains and their possessions, and in this way become the redeemed, messianic community of Christ the King.'
David Watson, Discipleship

Notes

Notes

SESSION TEN

What Next?

'God made people simple; people's complex problems are of their own devising' (Ecclesiastes 7:29).

Goals

- To reflect on the course and consider how it has impacted upon us, individually and as a group.
- To look at where to go from here.

Reading

'Only the simple are free. All others are tyrannised by the ambitious self, the demand for recognition through things and a preoccupation with the opinions of others.' Francois Fenelon declared, 'Simplicity is an uprightness of soul which prevents self-consciousness. Verily such simplicity is a great treasure!'
(Richard Foster, Celebration of Discipline, p.117)

'People choose their own prisons because they don't like the responsibilities that come with freedom. Because once you are free, you see the world as it is and you feel called to serve, to respond to the pain and confusion.'
(From Joe Dominguez, Yes!, Summer 1999)

'The plain fact is that we are starving people, not deliberately in the sense that we want them to die, but wilfully in the sense that we prefer their death to our inconvenience.'
(Victor Gollancz)

Over the past two or three months we have been meeting as a group to consider what it means to live a simpler lifestyle. We have discussed why it is important and how we can begin to adopt some of the principles ourselves. We have covered many issues and have left a number out (most notably the more inner dimensions of simplicity). What is certainly true is that a whole book could be written on each of the topics and each session has only served as a starting-block for what will be a lifetime's journey.

Because of the nature of the material, many of us will now need to take time to go over some of the particular areas that interested and challenged us: to go through the recommended reading and resources; to pray through our responses and talk with other people about how we will begin to grapple with these things. What is certain is that it could be all too easy for us to sit back and think 'we've done that' and forget all that we have been learning. We have just begun a journey. How will we ensure that we keep going along that path?

One of the best ways of making sure that we keep going in the right direction is through having a 'mission statement' for our lives.[79] Tom Sine tells of a friend of his, Jerry, who lost his wife and one of his children in a car accident, leaving him alone to bring up the other three. After weeks of praying and struggling with grief:

> ...it dawned on him that one of the ways to honour those who died was to sit down with his three children and write a family mission statement – to raise his children with a definite purpose in mind. He sat down with his three children

'A person is rich in proportion to the things he can leave along the way.'
Henri Thoreau

and, with his biblical training, drafted a family mission statement… . They check it every week to ensure they are finding creative ways to bring faith to every dimension of their life as a family. [80]

Generally speaking, a mission statement is a short phrase or sentence which provides a person or group of people with a sense of purpose for their life. It expresses what we believe to be the reason for our existence and it defines the focus for who we are and what we do (our 'calling'). Unlike the usual mission statements that corporations or individuals develop, they are centred on our relationship to God and our desire to do God's will rather than on our own personal happiness, dreams or ambitions. They are also outwardly focused on our relationships with others and the world around us rather than inwardly on the gratification of our own dreams and ambitions. Mission statements are a very good way to help us stay focused on the values we want our lives to be based upon.

So how do we go about writing one? Begin by taking a sheet of paper, or sitting down at your computer, and prayerfully make some jottings, listing words and ideas that you may want to include in the finished picture. As you make your list, try to stay clear of vague generalisations. 'To serve God' is not enough by itself. How is it to be achieved? When and where?

Here are a few ideas to think about as you jot down your words and thoughts:

- Think back over what you have learnt on this course and the effect it has had on your relationship with God and your understanding of his purposes for you.
- What do you sense God is nudging you towards in terms of your life's direction and priorities?
- What words or phrases from Scripture or elsewhere have struck you during this course?
- What has God been impressing upon you in your times of quiet with him or in prayer with others?
- What areas of human need most make you want to respond?
- What experiences (positive and negative) have you been through that God can use to make you more valuable to others?
- What gifts and abilities do you have that God may want to use in his service?
- What are you doing already that you sense God is pleased with?

Now we get to the creative part. This is a chance to allow our dreams and imaginations to run wild! Invite the Spirit of God to flow through you and reveal to you creative ways that everything you have written down so far could come together. Jot down the thoughts and dreams that come into your mind. Spend time in silence reflecting on what God has been saying to you. Write down any additional thoughts or impressions that come into your minds.

Now to the hard part. This is bringing together the passions of your heart and the desires of God for your life, into a single statement – a short, outwardly focused phrase or sentence that you feel reflects your emerging sense of purpose. If possible, incorporate Scripture in your statement and, above all, make sure that it reflects the issues of simplicity that you feel passionate about and what you believe should be at the centre of your life.

A few further pointers to help us along the way:

- Don't worry about getting it all done at once – it is more likely to be 'work in progress' that you will keep beavering away at.
- Don't try to include too much – we're writing a mission statement not a mission book!
- Make it simple and precise enough to memorise as you set out into the day.
- Make it inspirational so that it enthuses you whenever you look at it.

'All men dream, but not equally. Those who dream by night in the dusty recesses of their minds wake in the day to find it was vanity: but the dreamers of the day are dangerous men, for they may act their dream with open eyes to make it possible.'
Lawrence of Arabia

You could divide the statement into three: firstly, 'the reason I / we exist is to…'; secondly, 'the values I / we hold fast to are…'; thirdly, 'the goals I/we will set out to achieve are...'.

When a shape begins to emerge, check it out with one or two others whom you trust (or this group). Ask them for their honest evaluation and feedback.

Once we have our mission statement basically written we can decide how to use it. Maybe you will want to pray through it each week or bring it to a group of friends regularly to keep you accountable to it. Whatever we do, let us remember that the key to following our mission statements is prayer. Spend perhaps five minutes each morning with your diary and mission statement in front of you, and ask the simple question, 'So OK, God, what are you doing, and what do you want me to do today?' If we all did this it would revolutionise our lives and help us to live a life of simplicity with God at our centre.

Discussion

- What do you think the simple life means? How has your understanding of simplicity developed since you were first asked this question in Session One?
- What have been the main things you have enjoyed about this course?
- What are the things with which you have struggled?
- Are there any particular areas that you want to look at further and where you know there is still 'unfinished business'?
- At the start of this course we looked at the relationship between the inner reality of simplicity and the outer action. Have you been able to maintain that balance?
- How have you found this group? Do you in any way want to maintain the continuity and relationships that you have built up, or do you feel that the group has come to its useful and natural end?
- What do you think about the idea of creating your own mission statement? Will you do it?

Action and Homework

Write your own mission statement and begin to use it as a basis for your life.

Prayer

The following extract comes from the writings of a Catholic priest who works with the homeless in France:

> Lord, why did you tell me to love all people? I have tried, but I come back to you and I am frightened.
>
> I was so peaceful at home. I was so comfortably settled, it was well furnished and I felt cosy. I was at peace sheltered from the wind and the rain and the mud. And I would like to have stayed unsullied in my ivory tower. But you, Lord, have found a breach in my defences. You have forced me to open my door.
>
> Like a swash of rain in my face the cry of men has awakened me. Like a gale of wind a friendship has shaken me. As a ray of light slips in unnoticed, your grace has stirred me. And rationally enough, I left my door ajar. Now, Lord, I am lost, for outside people are lying in wait for me. I didn't know they were so near. As I started to open the door, I saw them with outstretched hands and burning eyes and longing hearts; like beggars on the church steps. The first ones came in, Lord; there was after all some space in my heart. I welcomed them – I would have cared for them and fondled

'What I needed was the solitude to expand in breadth and depth and to be simplified out under the gaze of God, more or less the way a plant spreads out its leaves in the sun.'
Thomas Merton, Seven Storey Mountain

them, my very own little lambs, my flock. You would have been so pleased with me, Lord. I would have served you and honoured you in a respectable way – it was sensible until then. But the next ones, Lord – and I hadn't seen them – they were hidden behind the first ones. There were more of them. They were wretched and they overpowered me.

Without warning we had to crowd in. I had to find room for them in my heart too. Now they've come from all over in successive waves, pushing one another, jostling one another, from all over town, all over the country, all over the world, numberless and inexhaustible. They don't come alone any longer but in groups bound to one another and bending under heavy loads, loads of injustice, resentment, hate, suffering, sin. And they drag the world behind them with everything rusted and twisted and badly adjusted. Lord, they hurt me. They are in the way. They are too hungry, and I can't do anything any more. They push the door to my heart and the door opens, but Lord, my door is as wide open as it can get – I can't stand it, it is too much, it is no kind of life. What about my job, my family, my peace, my liberty – what about me? There is no room for me any more.

'Don't worry, son, don't worry, my child. While people were coming to you, I, your father, your God, also slipped in among them.'

* * *

'Not that I have already obtained all this, or have already been made perfect, but I press on to take hold of that for which Christ Jesus took hold of me. Brothers and sisters, I do not consider myself yet to have taken hold of it. But one thing I do: forgetting what is behind and straining towards what is ahead, I press on towards the goal to win the prize for which God has called me heavenwards in Christ Jesus'
(Philippians 3:12–15).

'A remarkable piece of work, clearly the result of years of serious investigation into poverty and its causes... What I like most about it is that you get right down to the core of the issue from a biblical point of view, and the core is that I am the cause of poverty through my thoughtless, wasteful consumption habits, and so is everyone else.'

'The life of lies is made of strange stuff. As long as it seals off the entire society, it appears to be made of stone. But the moment someone breaks through in one place, when one person cries out "The Emperor is naked!" – when a single person breaks the rules of the game, thus exposing the game – everything suddenly appears in another light and the whole crust seems then to be made of a tissue on the point of tearing and disintegrating uncontrollably.'
Vaclav Havel, former president of the Czech republic, The Power of the Powerless

Notes

Notes

Appendix 1: Timesheet

Time	Monday	Tuesday	Wednesday	Thursday	Friday	Saturday	Sunday
7-8							
8-9							
9-10							
10-11							
11-12							
12-1							
1-2							
2-3							
3-4							
4-5							
5-6							
6-7							
7-8							
8-9							
9-10							
10-11							
11-12							
sleep							

Appendix 2: Time circles

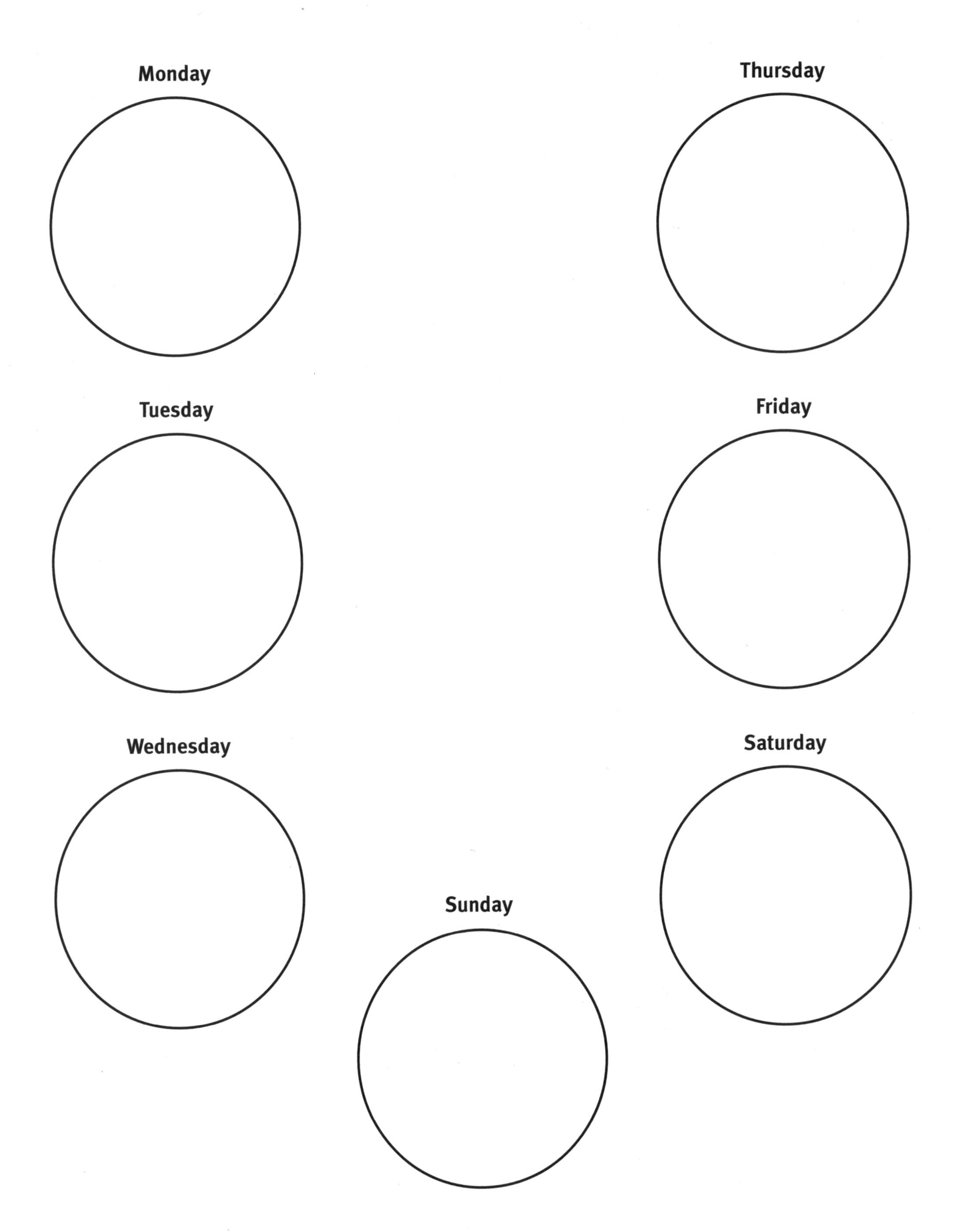

Appendix 3: Looking after your personal money

Here is a simple way to look after your personal money.
It does take a bit of discipline and time but it is well worth it in the long run!

1. What money do you have coming in?

a) Take the **Personal Money form** (on page 93), and go to the first table (with TOTAL COMING IN at the bottom). In the first column list all the sources of money you have coming in, including money coming in from your family, or anyone else with whom you share living costs (eg wages, IS, JSA, Family Credit and other benefits, maintenance, interest etc). There is a filled-in example attached to help you.

b) In the weekly columns, record the amount you receive from each source. At the end of each week add up the different sources to work out your total weekly amount coming in.

c) At the end of the month, work out how much you received from each source over the whole month and add them together. This figure is your TOTAL COMING IN this month.

2. What do you spend each day?

a) In a notebook, record the details of everything you buy (record it on the day you pay, regardless of how you pay). Include: rent, mortgage, childcare, appliance rental, hire purchase, mail order, credit cards, pension, travel expenses, food and drink, school, household bills, telephone, electricity, gas, water, clothes, tax, national insurance, other insurance, leisure activities, giving etc.

b) Record the date, what you bought and the price. If you have a receipt, you may want to keep it as a back-up record of the purchase.

3. What is your total monthly spending?

a) In the second table (with TOTAL SPENT at the bottom) fill in the names of all your expenses this month (eg Presents, Mail order bill, Children's pocket money).

b) Using what you have written in your notebook, fill in the amount spent each week on each item.

c) By adding up the total at the bottom of each weekly column you can see how you spend your money each week.

d) At the end of the month, calculate the total amount spent on each item by adding across the page. To work out how much you spend monthly add up the Total column. The number in the bottom right hand box is the total amount you have spent during the month.

4. How are you doing?

a) To calculate your Money left over use the third table, at the bottom of the page. First copy the TOTAL COMING IN line as indicated by the arrow. Next, do the same with the TOTAL SPENT line. Your Money left over is TOTAL COMING IN minus TOTAL SPENT. Simple!

b) You can also keep a Running total of how much you have left over after each week. Hopefully you will have some spare money left over at the end of the month. If the number is negative, then you have spent more than you have had coming in for this month. If this happens, you should look at what you spent to see if you could reduce it next month. The amount left over is the amount you have to go towards next month's budget.

5. Try an example

Look at the example of Mrs R. E. Joyce. See if you can understand how she keeps track of her personal money. Then try and do it for yourself!

Mrs Joyce, a single mother aged 29 with a daughter of 8 (Hope) has kept her accounts for August: as follows:

What came in

Month: August	Week 1 £	Week 2 £	Week 3 £	Week 4 £	Total £
Amount left over from last month	14.34				14.34
Income support (£54.65 weekly)	54.65	54.65	54.65	54.65	218.60
Dependent Child (£38.50 weekly)	38.50	38.50	38.50	38.50	154.00
Money earned by ironing	8.00	8.00	8.00	8.00	32.00
Gift from sister			50.00		50.00
Interest on savings account				0.75	0.75
Total coming in:	115.49	101.15	151.15	101.90	469.69

What you spent

	Week 1 £	Week 2 £	Week 3 £	Week 4 £	Total £
Giving	2.00	2.00	7.00	2.00	13.00
Saving *	5.00	5.00	5.00	5.00	20.00
Rent / Mortgage	11.00	11.00	11.00	11.00	44.00
Council Tax	-	-	-	-	0.00
Gas			12.00		12.00
Electricity	12.00				12.00
Water	-	-	-	-	0.00
Telephone	2.00	2.00	2.00	2.00	8.00
Food and drink	28.90	30.68	27.34	31.76	118.68
Newsagent	-	-	-	-	0.00
Toiletries	12.32				12.32
Laundry / Cleaning	-	-	-	-	0.00
Insurance	-	-	-	-	0.00
Transport expenses	4.00	3.20	3.40	2.40	13.00
Clothing / Shoes			34.99		34.00
School expenses	5.00				5.00
Child care					
Eating out / Social					
Savings for quarterly payments	2.00	2.00	2.00	2.00	8.00
Health / Dental		1.49			1.49
Presents				4.36	4.36
Entertainment		12.50	1.34	15.00	28.84
TV Licence stamps	2.00	2.00	2.00	2.00	8.00
Mail order bill				9.30	9.30
Equipment rental	-	-	-	-	0.00
Hope's pocket money	1.00	1.00	1.00	1.00	4.00
Total spent:	87.22	72.87	109.07	87.82	356.98

Personal Money - How are you doing?	Week 1 £	Week 2 £	Week 3 £	Week 4 £	Total £
Total coming in	115.49	101.15	151.15	101.90	469.69
Total spent	87.22	72.87	109.07	87.82	356.98
Money left over ('coming in' minus 'spent')	28.27	28.28	42.08	14.08	112.71
Running total:	28.27	56.55	98.63	112.71	

Mrs Joyce gives £2 to the church each week. In the third week when she was given £50 she gave an additional £5. Her other form of giving is to give time by cleaning the church offices and kitchen two mornings a week.

Personal Money form

What came in

Month:	Week 1 £	Week 2 £	Week 3 £	Week 4 £	Total £
Total coming in:					

What you spent

	Week 1 £	Week 2 £	Week 3 £	Week 4 £	Total £
Giving					
Saving					
Rent / Mortgage					
Council Tax					
Gas					
Electricity					
Water					
Telephone					
Food and drink					
Newsagent					
Toiletries					
Laundry / Cleaning					
Insurance					
Transport expenses					
Clothing / Shoes					
School expenses					
Child care					
Eating out / Social					
Total spent:					

Personal Money - How are you doing?	Week 1 £	Week 2 £	Week 3 £	Week 4 £	Total £
Total coming in					
Total spent					
Money left over ('coming in' minus 'spent')					
Running total:					

Appendix 4: What on earth am I doing? [81]

A personal lifestyle audit

Being a Christian should challenge us to face the issues of our world around us and do something about them. These questions provide a measure of checking out your lifestyle and thinking with reference to the environment. Your answers and scores should be a stimulus for discussion and action – mark yourself as honestly as you can! Use the definitions overleaf to clarify the questions.
Please tick a box for each question.

I BUY:	I do it	I think about it	It doesn't cross my mind
Fair Trade coffee			
Fair Trade tea			
Environmentally friendly washing powder/liquid			
Free range eggs			
Free range/organic meat/fruit/vegetables			
Milk from a milkman			
Items with less packaging (whenever possible)			
Items with less transport miles (when aware)			
Clothes/shoes from shops with an ethical policy			

I RECYCLE:			
Newspapers/waste paper			
Glass			
Aluminium or steel cans & plastic			
Garden waste on a compost heap			
Kitchen waste on a compost heap or in a wormery			
Clothes/books			

I MAKE A POINT OF USING:			
Local shops instead of supermarkets			
Local businesses instead of multinationals			
Local farmers' market and farm shops			
Public transport/car sharing			
A bike instead of a car			
A car with a small engine			
Energy-saving light bulbs and sava-plugs on my fridge/freezer			
Lights/electrical equipment & turn off when finished (not on stand-by)			
Produce which I have grown/made myself			
Recycled paper/envelopes/toilet and kitchen paper			
Gas and electricity from a green tariff			

I SUPPORT:	I do it	I think about it	It doesn't cross my mind
Local conservation groups			
National environmental organisations			
Birds, by providing food in my garden and putting bells on any cats I own.			
Local wildlife by gardening organically			
Banks with an ethical policy/ethical investments			
Each point is worth:	2	1	0
Grand total:	+	=	

SCORES & DEFINITIONS

0-20	Being a Christian doesn't impact upon your lifestyle or thinking much. Choose an issue which interests you and discover how you can make a difference.
21-40	You're thinking about making a difference, but getting around to it remains a challenge! It's time to do those things you've been putting off!
41-62	Your lifestyle reflects that you've made changes. Challenge yourself to find out more and keep going!

'Fair Trade' is a process which pays producers a good price for their labour, instead of a price which they are forced to accept just to stay in business. As a by-product, the goods are often produced in a more environmentally-friendly manner.

'Environmentally Friendly' means being sensitive to the need to reduce the use of natural resources, considering pollution and the amount of energy used by producing or using a product.

'Free Range' is a term applied to livestock which have continuous day time access to open air. The ground is mainly covered with vegetation, there is a maximum density of livestock per acre, and the feed must be free of animal products. Free range must not be confused with 'Farm Fresh' or 'Country Fresh' which could still involve factory farming methods.

'Transport Miles' refers to the mileage covered by an item from the producer of the raw ingredients to the shop floor. For example, a locally grown potato may travel to a washing centre, then to a distribution centre before it reaches your local superstore. The local market will sell it dirty direct from the farm! More transport is used and therefore more congestion and pollution is produced by shopping at superstores.

'Recycling' is the idea of using materials again. If an item cannot be re-used in its present form, it can be broken down and the materials used again. This process uses far less energy and natural resources than using raw materials each time.

A 'Wormery' is a plastic bin with a sealed lid, a sump and a tap to drain off collected liquid. Tiger worms will eat degradable kitchen waste, turning it into a rich compost. The liquid forms an excellent plant feed – home made Baby Bio!

'Multinationals' are huge global companies which provide jobs in many nations but which don't necessarily consider the environmental and local economic impact of their business.

'Car Sharing' makes use of spare places in cars when two or more people are travelling to the same destination at the same time. The pollution caused by car fumes damages the ozone layer (which protects us from harmful sun rays) as well as contributing to diseases such as asthma.

'Farmers' Markets' are markets where local producers can sell their goods direct to the customer. They must come from a thirty-mile radius and the stall has to be staffed by the actual producer. The produce is not only fresher, but often contains few chemicals. Less packaging and transportation is required which means there is less waste and fewer road journeys. Farmers' Markets also encourage people to try home-produced, regional, specialities.

'Bicycling' is a far more environmentally-friendly means of transportation than driving. For example, a bicycle can travel up to 1,037km on the energy equivalent of one litre of petrol (nearly 300mpg).

Further Sources of Information

Magazines and websites

Adbusters: www.adbusters.org
New Internationalist: www.newint.org
Simple Living Network: www.slnet.org
Sojourners: www.sojo.net
Yes! A Journal of Positive Futures: www.yesmagazine.org
Changing Lives – The Magazine of Christians against Poverty: www.CAPuk.org

Books and Other Written Material

James Allcock, Robert Innes and David Sheppard, God at Work Part II (Grove Booklets E96)

David Batstone, *Saving the Corporate Soul and (Who Knows?) Maybe Your Own* (Jossey-Bars, 2003).

Richard Bauckham and Trevor Hart, *Hope Against Hope: Christian Eschatology in Contemporary Context* (Dartman, Longman and Todd, 1999).

John Benton, *Christians in a Consumer Culture* (Christian Focus Publications, 1999).

R. J. Berry (ed.), *The Care of Creation: Focusing Concern and Action* (IVP, 2000)

Craig Blomberg, *Neither Poverty Nor Riches: a Biblical Theology of Possessions* (Apollos, 1999)

Mark A. Burch, *Simplicity* (New Society Publishers, 1995)

Mark A. Burch, *Simplicity Study Circles* (New Society Publishers, 1997)

Larry Burkett, *Debt-Free Living* (Moody Press, 1989)

Joe Domingues and Vicky Robin, *Your money or your Life: Transforming Your Relationship with Money and Achieving Financial Independence* (Penguin Books, 1992)

Graham Dow, A Christian Understanding of Daily Work (Grove Booklet P57)

Duane Elgin, *Voluntary Simplicity* (Quill, 1981)

Richard J. Foster, *Celebration of Discipline* (Hodder & Stoughton, 1999)

Richard J. Foster, *Freedom of Simplicity* (Harper Paperbacks, 1989)

John Goldingay and Robert Innes, God at Work Part I (Grove Booklet E94)

Colin Gunton, *Christ and Creation* (Paternoster, 1992)

Donald Kraybill, *The Upside-down Kingdom* (Marshalls Paperback, 1978)

Doris Janzen Lonacre, *Living More With Less* (Herald Press 1980)

Susan Meeker-Lowry, *Invested in the Common Good* (New Society Publisher, 1995)

Paul Mills, A Brief Theology of Time. Part 2: Resisting the Tyranny of Time (Cambridge Papers 11.4, 2002)

Paul Mills, Faith Versus Prudence? Christians and Financial Security (Cambridge Papers, 1995)

Paul Mills, Investing as a Christian (Cambridge Papers, June 1996)

Janet Luhrs, *The Simple Living Guide* (Broadway Books, 1997)

Michael Northcott, *The Environment and Christian Ethics* (SPCK, 1999)

Northwest Earth Institute, *Discussion Course on Voluntary Simplicity* (1997)

Lawrence Osborn, *Guardians of Creation: Nature in Theology and the Christian Life* (Apollos, 1993)

Jonathan Sacks, *Faith in the Future* (Dartman, Longman and Todd, 1995)

E. F. Schumacher, *Small is Beautiful: a Study of Economics as if People Really Mattered* (Vintage 1993)

Michael Lloyd, (forthcoming work to be published by Alpha International)

Michael Schut (ed.), *Simpler Living:Compassionate Life: a Christian Perspective* (Living the Good News, 1999)

Ron J. Sider, *Rich Christians in an Age of Hunger* (Hodder and Stoughton, 1997)

Ron J. Sider, ed., *Lifestyle in the Eighties: An Evangelical Commitment to Simple lifestyle* (London, Paternoster, 1981.)

Ray Simpson, *Exploring Celtic Christianity* (Hodder & Stoughton, 1995)

Tom and Christine Sine, *Living on Purpose: Finding God's Best for Your Life* (Monarch, 2002)

Tom Sine, *Mustard Seed Vs. McWorld: Reinventing Christian Life for a New Millenium* (Monarch, 1999)

The Soil Association, *Local Food for Local People* (July 1998)

Mike Starkey, *Born to Shop* (Monarch, 1989)

Joseph Stiglitz, *Globalization and its Discontents* (Penguin, 2003)

John Stott, *New Issues Facing Christians Today* (Marshall Pickering, 1990)

Alan Storkey, *Transforming Economics* (SPCK, 1986)

Keith Tondeur, *Financial Tips for the Family: an Essential Guide* (Hodder & Stoughton, 1997)

Keith Tondeur, *What Jesus said about Money and Possessions* (Monarch Books 1998)

Keith Tondeur, *Your Money and Your Life* (Triangle, 1996)

Ruth Valerio, *L is for lifestyle: Christian Living that Doesn't Cost the Earth* (IVP, 2004 forthcoming)

Jean Vanier, *Community and Growth* (Dartman, Longmann and Todd Ltd, 1996)

John Wesley, *Wesley's 52 Standard Sermons* (Schmul Publishers, 1988)

World Development Movement, *The Good Life: your guide to everyday actions which ensure a fairer deal for the world's poor* (1998)

Notes

[1] John Stott, *New Issues Facing Christians Today* (Marshall Pickering, 1990), p.230.

[2] John Stott (ed.), *Making Christ Known* (Paternoster, 1996), p.142. / www.lausanne.org

[3] Papers that were presented at the consultation can be read in: Ron Sider, *lifestyle in the Eighties: An Evangelical Commitment to Simple lifestyle* (Paternoster, 1981).

[4] Janet Luhrs, *The Simple Living Guide* (Broadway, 1997), p.210.

[5] Quoted in Ron Sider, *lifestyle in the Eighties* (Paternoster, 1981), p.11.

[6] For a broader theological basis for simplicity, see Ruth Valerio, *Simplicity: Living Life to the Full.*

[7] Richard Foster, *Celebration of Discipline* (Hodder & Stoughton, 1999), p.107. Reproduced by permission of Hodder & Stoughton Limited.

[8] Richard Foster, *Celebration of Discipline* (Hodder & Stoughton, 1999), p.99.

[9] Richard Foster, *Celebration of Discipline* (Hodder & Stoughton, 1999), pp.110–115.

[10] Juliet Schor, quoted in Michael Schut (ed.), *Simpler Living* (Thomas More Press, 1999), pp.34–35.

[11] Tom Sine, *Mustard Seed Vs. McWorld: Reinventing Christian Life for a New Millennium* (Monarch, 1995), p.128.

[12] Story Songs Ltd. Sung by Harry Chapin.

[13] Roy McCloughry, 'Community Ethics' in *New Dictionary of Christian Ethics and Pastoral Theology* (IVP, 1995), 110.

[14] Michael Schut (ed.), *Simpler Living:Compassionate Life* (Thomas More Press, 1999), p.253.

[15] Michael Schut (ed.), *Simpler Living:Compassionate Life* (Thomas More Press, 1999), pp.50–51.

[16] Henri Nouwen, 'Contemplation and Ministry' quoted in Michael Schut (ed.), *Simpler Living:Compassionate Life* (Thomas More Press, 1999), p.54.

[17] Cited in, Doris Janzen Longacres, *Living More With Less* (Herald, 1980), p.75.

[18] Paul Mills, A brief theology of time. Part 2: Resisting the tyranny of time, Cambridge Papers 11:4, The Jubilee Centre, 2002. To obtain a copy phone the Jubilee Centre on 01223 501631 or see www.jubilee-centre.org

[19] Taken from T. Sine, *Mustard Seed Vs. McWorld: Reinventing Christian Life for a New Millenium* (Monarch, 1995), pp.238–239.

[20] Adapted from Mark A. Burch's study in *Simplicity* (New Society Publishers, 1993), pp.72–74.

[21] E.M.Forster, *Howard's End*, (Penguin, 1969), p.72.

[22] Craig Blomberg, *Neither Poverty Nor Riches: A Biblical Theology of Possessions* (IVP, 2001), p.83.

[23] Ron Sider, *lifestyle in the Eighties: An Evangelical Commitment to Simple lifestyle* (Paternoster, 1981), p.6.

[24] Craig Blomberg, *Neither Poverty Nor Riches: A Biblical Theology of Possessions* (IVP, 2001), pp.61–71.

[25] Donald B. Kraybill, *The Upside-down Kingdom* (Herald, 1991), pp.114–129.

[26] The Message translation of the Bible gives an excellent re-reading of this passage – well worth looking at if you have a copy. Eugene H. Peterson (ed.), The Message (NavPress, 2002).

[27] Hengel, 'Property and Riches in the Early Church', in *Earliest Christianity* (SCM Press, 1979), p.232.

[28] 2002 Report from the New Policy Institute (with support from the Joseph Rowntree Foundation).

[29] See Donald B. Kraybill, *The Upside-down Kingdom* (Herald, 1991) pp.152–155 for a fuller explanation of this.

[30] John Wesley, Sermon 29 in *Wesley's 52 Standard Sermons* (Schmul Publishing).

[31] Taken from, Michael Schut (ed.), *Simpler Living:Compassionate Life* (Thomas More Press, 1999), p.260.

[32] Adapted from Mark A. Burch, *Simplicity* (New Society Publishers, 1993), p.88.

[33] Much of the material in this session also appears in Ruth Valerio, *The Alphabet lifestyle,* Chapter 14: 'N is for Needs'.

[34] T. and C. Sine, *Living on Purpose: Finding God's Best for Your Life* (Monarch, 2002), pp.138–139.

[35] This is dependent on the world situation. In times of war, or increased instability, the arms trade is the biggest industry.

[36] World Tourist Organisation (WTO). 'Tourist arrivals' is the term used to measure tourism.

[37] Association of British Tourist Associations.

[38] John Stott, *Issues Facing Christians Today* (Marshall Pickering, 1984), p.166.

[39] Taken from Dominguez and Robin, *Your Money or Your Life* (Penguin, 1999), pp.229–230.

[40] Taken from his autobiography published 1984.

[41] Oxford English Dictionary.

[42] For those interested in looking at this further, two good books on capitalism are: Robert Heilbroner, The Nature and Logic of Capitalism (Norton and Co. 1985) and Bob Goudzwaard, Capitalism and Progress: A Diagnosis of Western Society (Paternoster, 1997).

[43] N. Myers, 'Environmental Refugees in a globally warmed world' (BioScience, v.43, 1993), pp.167–168. While these are the figures generally stated, there is debate over the extent of the environmental refugee problem among governments, NGOs and in academia. To read the other side, see R. Black, Environmental refugees: myth or reality?

[44] These four points are taken from Shantilal Bhagat, "Healing Ourselves and the Earth", in Michael Schut (ed.) *Simpler Living* (Thomas More Press, 1999).

[45] Shantilal Bhagat, 'Healing Ourselves and the Earth', in Michael Schut (ed.) Simpler Living (Thomas More Press, 1999).

[46] For a more in-depth theological treatment of this subject, for which there is not the space here, see M. Northcott, *The Environment and Christian Ethics* (Cambridge University Press, 1996) and L. Osborn, *Guardians of Creation* (Apollos, 1993).

[47] For more on this, see C. Wright, *Living as the People of God* (IVP, 1983), pp.68–69.

[48] Hughes, *God of the Poor* (Authentic lifestyle, 1998), p.301.

[49] The following paragraphs are taken from R. Valerio, *The Alphabet lifestyle* (forthcoming).

[50] Michael Lloyd, *Café Theology* (Alpha International, 2005), pp.28-29.

[51] R. Bauckham and T. Hart, *Hope Against Hope* (Darton, Longman & Todd Ltd, 1999), p.137.

[52] C. Gunton, *Christ and Creation* (Paternoster, 1992), p.64.

[53] It is interesting to note, also, that Jesus' resurrection body is both in continuity and discontinuity with his old body and is both physical and spiritual as he eats fish yet walks through walls.

[54] Adapted from Mark A. Burch, *Simplicity* (New Society Publishers, 1993), p.85.

[55] To look further into this, see J. Stiglitz, *Globlization and its Discontents* (Penguin, 2003). See also the relevant chapters in Ron Sider, *Rich Christians in an Age of Hunger* (Hodder & Stoughton, 1978) and D. Hughes, *God of the Poor* (Authentic Lifestyle, 1998) plus Alan Storkey, *Transforming Economics* (SPCK, 1996), E. F. Schumacher, *Small is Beautiful: a Study of Economics as if People Really Mattered* (Vintage, 1993) and Colin Hines, *Globalization: A Global Manifesto* (Earthscan 2000)

[56] D. Batstone, *Saving the Corporate Soul*, p.11. Copyright © D. Batstone 2003. Reprinted by permission of John Wiley & Sons Inc.

[57] Much of the material here is taken from Paul Mills' excellent paper Faith Versus Prudence? Christians and Financial Security, Cambridge Papers 4:1 (The Jubilee Centre, 1995). To obtain a copy phone the Jubilee Centre on 01223 566319 or see www.jubilee-centre.org

[58] Ibid pp.3–4.

[59] Larry Burkett, *Debt-free Living* (Moody Press, 1999), p.57.

[60] Credit Action: 01223 324034; www.creditaction.com.

[61] Taken from Keith Tondeur, *Financial Tips for the Family*, pp.58–59.

[62] From an unpublished paper entitled, Tithing: Biblically Non-Christian? See also R.T. Kendall, *The Gift of Giving* (Hodder & Stoughton, 1982).

[63] To look further at the question of interest, see Paul Mills, *The Ban on Interest*, Cambridge Papers 3:1(The Jubilee Centre, 1993).

[64] To explore this further, see *The Wheat Economy* available from FACE to Face.

[65] See Paul Mills, Investing as a Christian Cambridge Papers 7:6 (The Jubilee Centre, 1996) for a helpful look at the current investment options (eg Banks, National Savings, shares etc) in the light of some of these principles.

[66] The Besom Foundation and FACE to Face provide some practical ways of beginning to outwork this. Contact them for more details. www.besom.com

[67] Paul Mills, Investing as a Christian, Cambridge Papers 7:6 (The Jubilee Centre, 1996), p.1.

[68] The World Development Movement's *The Good Life* is a good place to start for further information.

[69] Burkett, *Debt-free Living* (Moody Press, 1989) p.142.

[70] Ron Sider, *Lifestyle in the Eighties: An Evangelical Commitment to a Simple Lifestyle* (Paternoster, 1981), p.9.

[71] Taken from Fusion cell notes material: Issue 8, 2000, p.33.

[72] These examples have been taken from Ray Simpson, *Exploring Celtic Spirituality* (Hodder & Stoughton, 1995), pp.37–38.

[73] Esther de Waal, *The Celtic Vision* (Dartman Longman and Todd, 1988), p.12.

[74] Ray Simpson, *Exploring Celtic Spirituality* (Hodder & Stoughton, 1995), pp.195–201.

[75] From Racial Justice Sunday pack, 2002.

[76] J. Sacks, *Faith in the Future* (Dartman, Longman and Todd, 1995), p.78.

[77] Taken from the Co-housing Network website: www.cohousing.co.uk

[78] Ray Simpson, *Exploring Celtic Spirituality* (Hodder & Stoughton, 1995), p.42.

[79] Much of the following has been adapted from Tom and Christine Sine's material in *Mustard Seed Vs McWorld*, Fusion cell notes issue 8 and the Spring Harvest 1999 Study Guide.

[80] T. Sine, *Mustard Seed Vs. McWorld: Reinventing Christian Life for a New Millenium* (Monarch, 1995), p.281.

[81] This lifestyle audit has been adapted by R. Valerio from original material by Chris Seaton and Clare Elkington.